SOJOURNER'S
WORKBOOK

A Guide to Thriving Cross-Culturally

CONNIE BEFUS, PH.D.

Sojourner's Workbook: A Guide to Thriving Cross-Culturally
by Connie Befus

Copyright © 2018, Connie Befus
ISBN: 978-0-9899545-7-0

Editorial Team: Joan Wilcox, Megan Munoz and Patty Woodyard

Cover Design: Jason LaBombard

BottomLine Media is a publishing imprint of Pioneers-USA, 10123 William Carey Dr., Orlando, FL 32832

Contents

Acknowledgments

I WOULD LIKE TO EXPRESS my thanks to Joan Wilcox, Megan Munoz and Patty Woodyard, my editorial team at Pioneers. Their input was invaluable in making this workbook more readable, relevant and user friendly. It was a pleasure to work with them.

Special thanks to Joan Wilcox, in particular, who not only served as editor and editorial liaison, but who was also an instigator and advocate for getting the *Sojourner Workbook* published. If this workbook is helpful for international workers, significant credit accrues to Joan.

Finally, deep thanks to the many international workers who have shared with me, over the years, their struggles, stress and joys in crossing cultures. Their lives and stories have enriched me and laid the groundwork for this workbook. May their process of learning to thrive be an ongoing blessing to others.

Connie Befus, December 2017

Why I Write for Sojourners

I HAVE BEEN A SOJOURNER IN SIX COUNTRIES—and have reveled in the enjoyable parts of those adventures. I have also experienced firsthand the stress, loneliness, and fatigue of being a stranger in a strange land. I have used that experience, and my training as a psychologist, to help other sojourners in their adjustment process.

Early in my counseling career, while living overseas, I pondered the difficulties so many expatriates experience in adapting to a foreign country, and asked, "Does it have to be so hard? Might there be ways to make cross-cultural adjustment easier?"

I was especially interested in making it easier for people who follow Jesus Christ and seek to live as His disciples. It concerned me to see these people struggle in the process of adjusting to their foreign country and sometimes fail, returning home discouraged and defeated.

So when I had the opportunity to do research as part of my doctoral program in counseling psychology, I chose to study "culture shock."* As part of my study, I devised ways of making the adjustment process easier, and sojourners more effective. What I learned from doing that research, plus what I have learned since, is shared with you in this workbook.

chapter 1

Introduction to Sojourning

Sojourners are people who voluntarily leave their homeland to live in a foreign country for a significant period of time, for reasons strong enough to make them embrace the challenges— as well as the enjoyment—involved.

Sojourning Is an Adventure!

BEING A SOJOURNER REQUIRES a courageous spirit, perseverance, and flexibility. Parts of sojourning are very enjoyable, while other parts can be downright difficult. If you are a sojourner, I doubt you'll need help with the enjoyable aspects of sojourning, but like the sojourners below, you might profit from encouragement and coaching:

> On a trip to Africa, I met with a young couple—Dan and Wendy—who had been in their new country six months. They were exhausted and struggling. "I can't get enough sleep," Wendy said. "My two-year-old has nightmares every night and wants to sleep with me. It's so hot … The mosquitoes get in, in spite of the screens … It takes me ages to cook because everything has to be made from scratch."

> Due to the Wendy's fatigue, Dan was doing most of the child care, cleaning, and errands. Neither of them was getting language study or work done.

> "What is the matter with this country?" demanded Dan irritably. "The electricity goes off with no warning; half the time there's no water. We can't bathe or wash clothes. I can't get an internet connection. I stood in line for visa papers for three days—and still don't have them!"

Wendy cried on a daily basis; Dan was tense and angry. Both felt like failures. I listened to them sympathetically, knowing their stress and complaints were very real.

I explained to this young couple that what they were experiencing is a normal part of being a sojourner. I encouraged them to adjust their expectations, and shared coping skills for survival.

•••

Marla was in her first months in an Asian country. No one near her spoke her native language, and she wrote me, asking if the anxiety and weariness she was experiencing were normal. I responded immediately, inviting her to discuss her symptoms with me by phone or e-mail and assuring her that some anxiety and fatigue are indeed part of cross-cultural adjustment. For several months we maintained a dialogue in which I affirmed the good sense and courage Marla exhibited and made suggestions for how she could handle stress, reduce fatigue, and build relationships.

I saw Dan and Wendy[1] four years later in their home country. They were eagerly looking forward to returning to Africa: they had learned to survive, then to thrive, and were enthusiastically invited to return to their adopted country by both expatriate and host country colleagues. Marla is now doing well. It was not easy, but she adapted to the customs of her adopted country and made friends. She moved from struggling to surviving to thriving.

Are you a sojourner? In what ways has your experience been like the early months for Dan, Wendy, and Marla?

_____

_____

_____

It is common to struggle in the early months of sojourning. But there are ways to make the experience easier; there are tried and true techniques for maintaining good health and adapting well to a foreign culture. The techniques and suggestions I shared with Dan, Wendy, and Marla comprise the content of this workbook written for sojourners.

What a Sojourner Is—and Isn't

A sojourner is not a refugee fleeing problems in their home country. A sojourner is not an immigrant, seeking permanent citizenship in the new country. Sometimes sojourns are brief, but technically a sojourner is not a tourist—sampling a country as recreation. A sojourner is not a short-term visitor: sojourning involves *residing* in a country, *as a temporary home*, usually for years. Therefore it involves adapting well enough to maintain good health, build amicable relationships, and enjoy the host culture and function in it effectively—*not merely tolerate it.*

A short visit to a foreign country is not necessarily life changing—but sojourning is, because it expands our experience, broadens our minds, deepens our souls, and challenges us to the cores of our beings. It forces us to dig deep into ourselves for strengths we didn't know we had—or don't have, and therefore must learn.

Sojourning well demands that we listen, question our assumptions, and walk in the shoes of a strange people.

In sojourning, we are the alien. Resident, but always alien. Since we are the alien and guest, we must tread carefully and not offend. We must learn how our hosts think and why their customs matter. We must adapt to them with respect and courtesy, yet not abandon who we are and our reason for sojourning there.

Even as we engage in all that adapting, there is much we have left behind, so we have losses, loneliness, and stress.

Sojourning can be enjoyable, valuable, and deeply meaningful—but is not for the faint of heart.

> *Sojourning well demands that we listen, question our assumptions, and walk in the shoes of a strange people.*

The Risks

A man sits in a bus station swallowing hard and blinking back tears. He is in his thirties, but looks worn out. He needs to get on a bus and get home, but he is not sure which bus. He thinks he knows the right words to ask someone, but he is not sure he will understand the rapid Spanish he will get in return. He's not sure he can handle the crowded bus either: the smells of sweat and garlic, the noise, the diesel fumes. Also, he dreads getting home to tell his wife the package did not come, and the medicine she asked for is not available ... he tried six pharmacies.

It's getting dark and starting to rain; he needs to gather his courage and find the bus. If only there were a bus that said, "Elkhart, Indiana"—he'd be on it in a heartbeat. He sighs and thinks, "Good thing there isn't one. I'd be out of here."

Success as a sojourner cannot be assumed.

Some sojourners flounder because stress symptoms undermine their mental or physical health and cause them to depart for medical reasons. Other sojourners manage the stress, but do not adapt to the culture or build effective relationships. They then leave in frustration, critical of the country they had meant to adopt as their new home. Or perhaps worse—they stay in the foreign country, leaking negative vibes. *Not* the desired result.

This workbook is designed to prevent those negative outcomes, and help sojourners maneuver from surviving to thriving. A sojourner can journey through this time well by practicing the seven tasks below. A more thorough explanation of each goal, with practical recommendations for building ongoing resilience, will be provided in the remaining chapters of this book.

The Seven Goals of the First Year of Sojourn

1. Manage stress in the midst of huge change: accumulation of many changes and transitions causes stress early in a sojourn. Chapter 2 describes how to manage current symptoms and prevent chronic stress.

2. Grieve the losses involved in leaving home: family, friends, church, familiar foods, parks, shops, roads, and services. Do such losses actually need to be *mourned?* Yes, they do, and if they are not effectively mourned, the result can be depression and resentment. How to do the grieving is explained in Chapter 3.

3. Build positive recreation patterns into your new life. While a new sojourner might feel such things have been sacrificed, Chapter 4 explains the importance of not sacrificing everything.

4. Develop healthy patterns of rest and play. New sojourners are notorious for burning the candle at both ends, or for not knowing how to rest and play for healthy restoration. There are good reasons why this is so. Chapter 5 explains those reasons and provides practical suggestions for avoiding burnout.

5. Chapter 6 will help you retrain the brain. The brain has *so* much to learn in the first year of a sojourn! It is wise, then, to be a good steward of your brain as it is retrained in learning hundreds of new thinking patterns, and in becoming aware of subtle and mysterious paradigms that undergird the new culture.

6. Resolve identity issues. Many sojourners find that in their new country they are not "who they used to be," nor "who they thought they would become." They did not know that reconfiguring one's identity is part of successful cross-cultural adjustment. Chapter 7 probes the identity issues involved in sojourning and provides guidance for moving toward an appropriate identity.

7. Maintain and deepen spiritual transformation. It sounds basic, but in fact, spiritual nurture and disciplines are often left behind in the throes of change. While letting go of spiritual disciplines while under stress is understandable, it is also lethal. Chapter 8 suggests feasible ways to maintain spiritual life during times of stress and change.

Success in Sojourning

A man sits in the airport lounge waiting for his flight, swallowing hard and blinking back tears. His hair is white, his face lined and tanned. The lump in his throat and the tears occur as he remembers the hundreds of people who thronged the good-bye party held for him and his wife in their rural church. Hundreds and hundreds of people—all of whom he knew. Well, he had vaccinated their cows and birthed their lambs out in their fields. He had sat with them through deaths and funerals, and gone to countless birthday parties and baptisms. He grinned as he remembered sharing God's Word in stables and dirt-floored kitchens and preaching under a tree. So many had come to a living faith. But how astonishing: how many of them there were! And the love and gratitude they had expressed! He felt so overwhelmed.

His wife nudged him and said, "Flight is boarding, Hon. I can't believe you're actually going to retire … Are you really ready to go back to Elkhart, Indiana?"

Early in his sojourn, the man on the bus was ready to head home to Elkhart, Indiana, if given half a chance. But he and his wife persevered; they worked at, and accomplished, the seven goals of sojourning. Thirty-five years later, they have learned a deep love for their adopted country and its people—and are deeply loved in return.

I know many sojourners like that couple from Indiana: veterans who have learned resilience and adapted so beautifully to their adopted countries that they are honored and mourned when it is time for them to "go home." They leave behind them a rich legacy of faith, vibrantly alive in what had been, for them, an alien place, but became a second home and place of rich ministry.

Such can be your trajectory as well, if you accomplish the seven goals of a sojourner's first year.

How to Use This Workbook

Interactive format:

This book is designed to be interactive. You will periodically be invited to think about your past or current life and *write down your responses.* That's why it's called a *workbook.*

You may be tempted not to write anything down, but just keep on reading. I would be! And if that is what works best for you—go ahead. It's your book, your mind, your adjustment process.

But the writing assignments are designed to help you stop, think, and *apply* what is suggested.

It is absolutely critical that you apply what you learn from this workbook *now*—because the attitudes and behavior patterns you establish in the beginning of your sojourn are the ones you will stick with for years to come.

It is much harder to change thinking and behavior patterns after they have been engraved in your brain and body.

Unproductive or negative patterns that harm your success as a sojourner are easy to fall into—if you aren't aware of the helpful patterns you need to practice instead. Thus it is essential for you to learn the healthy patterns described in the seven goals—and practice them—as early in your sojourn as you can. Establishing healthy patterns now will help you:

1. Survive the first difficult months of being a sojourner
2. Build resilience that will help you sojourn long and well

It is much harder to change thinking and behavior patterns after they have been engraved in your brain and body.

Chapter order

I recommend a sojourner read Chapter 1 in the first month or two of sojourning, then read Chapter 2 right away and begin to follow the suggestions. It may take two, three, or four weeks for a sojourner to practice and benefit from the skills taught in each chapter. When those skills are becoming helpful and habitual, the sojourner can move on to the next chapter.

But life does not follow ideal patterns, as I'm sure you've noticed. The needs of early sojourning do not sequence themselves nicely: they overlap, combine, and repeat in new permutations. So read the chapters as you need them—in whatever order works for you.

And don't be surprised if you read a chapter once, but find you need to go back and digest it again. Many of the recommendations and techniques provided are skills: it takes time and practice to perfect skills.

Learning how to survive and thrive will be a work in progress—for some time to come.

End Game

If you find the process of cross-cultural adaptation arduous at times, be comforted: evidence suggests that those who feel the pain the most end up being more effective in the long haul.[2]

Be patient with yourself. Give yourself time to read, learn, think, pray, and practice the skills provided in this workbook.

It is my hope and prayer that you will persevere, accomplish the seven goals, and become one of those sojourners, like so many I know, who build healthy lives and adapt to their adopted country so well that they become deeply loved and highly effective ambassadors of hope.

Footnotes

1. Names used in this workbook will not be the real names of people described, but the stories are taken from real life and real people.

2. "The conclusion that the best behaviors for cultural adaptation and successful inter-action are also those that are likely to bring about culture shock was substantiated in a study by Ruben and Kealey (1979). The authors found that "persons who were most aware of the personal and subjective nature of their perceptions, knowledge, values, biases, and so on, experienced the most intense culture shock...

   ...It may be that in some cases at least, the persons who will ultimately be most ef-fective can be expected to undergo the most intense culture shock during transition." Brent Ruben and Daniel Kealey quoted in *Handbook of Intercultural Training, Vol. II,* p.40. Dan Landis, Richard W. Brislin. Pergamon Press, 1983.

chapter 2

Jars of Clay: Managing Stress in Fragile Containers

But we have this treasure in jars of clay to show that this all-surpassing power is from God and not from us.
—2 Corinthians 4:7 (NIV)

W̲E ARE ISSUED ONE JAR in which to carry the treasure. Only one.

In Biblical times there were no bank deposit vaults, no steel safes, no aluminum boxes, no locks and keys. Small valuables, expensive liquid, and important parchments were kept in ceramic jars. Jars made of clay.

We human beings are made from clay. So when the Apostle Paul says, "We have this treasure in jars of clay," he is using a beautiful metaphor to convey the fact that as we seek to share the Good News about Jesus, we carry the treasure of the Gospel in the fragile clay jars of our bodies.

In some ways these bodies of ours are remarkably resilient. On the other hand, they are incredibly fragile.

Because we are given only one body in which to carry this valuable treasure, we need to take care of it, and learn to manage the stress that comes with cross-cultural sojourning.

It is important to keep in mind that we need to take care of ourselves, not out of self-centeredness, nor an idealization of "physical fitness," but because our bodies are temples of the Holy Spirit—and the way God has chosen to share His treasure.

Being a Sojourner Is Inherently Stressful

Stress management is especially needed in the early months of a sojourn overseas because whether we're moving from Montana to Miami, or Miami to China, our bodies feel the stressful effects of multiple changes.

First there's jet lag to recover from. Then, there is often more noise—or different noise—in a new environment. We need more sleep, yet can't sleep well. The climate or altitude may be hard to adapt to. Our digestive systems react to different water, new foods, and new microorganisms, and sometimes revolt in the process. Meanwhile, we expect our brains to cope with an astonishing array of new information, new stimuli, and multiple decisions.

If you, as a new sojourner, feel stressed, that is completely understandable.

Stress Is Not Bad

It is important to remember that stress in itself is not necessarily bad. Stress is simply the way our bodies react to change—change of any kind: desirable or dreadful. Our bodies react with heightened adrenaline for a wedding, a birthday party, or giving a presentation. Our bodies also get into high gear if we are attacked, hit by a natural disaster, or are helping others in a crisis.

We aren't designed to stay in high gear.

This reaction to change or threat is not a sin or weakness. God made us this way, so that we can quickly move into high gear in response to an immediate need for action. It can even be enjoyable to experience that jolt of adrenaline and be in high gear!

Most of us can sustain a high level of adrenaline and energy output for three or four days and still function well. But stress that goes on longer than three or four days does damage to our systems. We are made to gear up with the stress response for short periods, but then return to lower gear.

We aren't designed to stay in high gear.

Can We Be Called to Be Stressed?

Do you think we are sometimes called to be stressed? Called into high gear? If our adrenaline spikes for a preaching engagement, for an intense three-day event, or because we are helping others in a crisis, such actions may be exactly what God wants us doing at that point in time, and adrenaline gives us the energy to do them.

At other times, though, chronic stress is our own fault, the result of bad stewardship.

Our stress symptoms can be the result of our own bad planning or our need to feel indispensable and stay in high gear. At such times, stress is not the result of obedience but occurs because we are addicted to our own adrenaline or sense of importance.

Managing stress is a spiritual discipline.

When we blast ahead, assuming our hard work is more important than anything else, we don't take time to consider what God wants for us. We need to frequently ask ourselves, and the Lord, if experiencing certain stressors is necessary out of obedience. Or would it be better stewardship to give our clay jars some downtime?

"To obey is better than sacrifice" (1 Samuel 15:22).

Managing stress is a spiritual discipline.

How Much Stress Have You Piled Up?

By the time a typical sojourner is several months into their sojourn—after packing, good-byes, flights, arriving overseas, and then more adjustments—it is common for them to experience the effects of cumulative stress.

So how much stress have you piled up?

Below you will find a list of typical stress symptoms. Please read through the list and put a check by each of the symptoms you have experienced in the past month. Put two checks by those you have experienced often or severely.

- ☐ fatigue
- ☐ irritability
- ☐ digestive upset
- ☐ negative attitude
- ☐ crying
- ☐ sense of numbness
- ☐ lack of concentration
- ☐ compulsive thoughts
- ☐ discomfort with strangers
- ☐ depression
- ☐ headaches

- ☐ low self-esteem
- ☐ muscle tension
- ☐ sleepiness
- ☐ complaining
- ☐ anxiety
- ☐ forgetfulness
- ☐ indecisiveness
- ☐ worrying
- ☐ lethargy
- ☐ sadness
- ☐ restlessness

☐ insomnia   ☐ backache

☐ paranoia   ☐ malaise

☐ others: _____

If you have checked any items above, know that it is possible to reduce or eliminate these symptoms by practicing stress management techniques that will be explained shortly.

But first, if you'd like to get an idea of how the stress of your last few months has added up, you can take a quick test that quantifies how much stress you have accumulated in the past year. It is called the Holmes-Rahe Stress Test and was developed years ago by researchers who noticed that individuals who experienced chronic stress showed a tendency to become ill.

Holmes and Rahe theorized that chronic or multiple stressors weakened the immune system. They therefore designed the test to match common stressors with a predictable likelihood of reduced immune system function and subsequent illness.[1]

Put a check next to each life event you have experienced *in the past 12 months*. Then add up your total.

Holmes-Rahe Stress Test

☐ Death of spouse, 100

☐ Divorce, 73

☐ Marital separation, 65

☐ Jail term, 63

☐ Death of close family member, 63

☐ Personal injury or illness, 53

☐ Marriage, 50

☐ Fired from work, 47

☐ Marital reconciliation, 45

☐ Retirement, 45

☐ Change in family member health, 44

☐ Pregnancy, 40

☐ Sex difficulties, 39

☐ Addition to family, 39

☐ Business readjustment, 39

☐ Trouble with in-laws, 29

☐ Son/daughter leaving home, 29

☐ Outstanding personal achievement, 28

☐ Spouse begins or ends work, 26

☐ Starting or finishing school, 26

☐ Change in living conditions, 25

☐ Revision of personal habits, 24

☐ Trouble with boss, 23

☐ Change in work hours, conditions, 20

☐ Change in residence, 20

☐ Change in schools, 20

☐ Change in recreational habits, 19

☐ Change in church activities, 19

☐ Change in social activities, 18

☐ Mortgage or loan under $10,000, 18

☐ Change in financial status, 38   ☐ Change in sleeping habits, 16

☐ Death of a close friend, 37   ☐ Change in # of family gatherings, 15

☐ Change in # of marital arguments, 35   ☐ Change in eating habits, 15

☐ Mortgage or loan over $10,000, 31   ☐ Vacation, 13

☐ Foreclosure of mortgage/loan, 30   ☐ Christmas season, 12

☐ Change in work responsibilities, 29   ☐ Minor violation of the law, 11

TOTAL: _____

Holmes and Rahe were not thinking about sojourners, and did not include such stressors as changing time zones, learning a new language, dealing in multiple currencies, or waiting for visas. Therefore we can assume that your stress score is probably higher than whatever total you just wrote down.

Note that according to Holmes and Rahe's research, a score over 300 indicates an 80 percent chance of illness. But, there are proactive things sojourners can do to counteract stress.

Of course, that is the point of having you fill out both of the above checklists: to help you realize how much stress you have experienced in recent months and remind you *that you need to take care of yourself.*

How to Manage Stress as a Sojourner

There are six things you can do to effectively manage stress as a sojourner:

1. Get enough sleep
2. Add a little exercise
3. Add simple activities that refresh and bring joy
4. Manage connections from back home
5. Use two simple techniques: deep breathing and progressive muscle relaxation
6. Prayerfully manage the *pacing* of your life

Before we go into how you can put these six stress management techniques into practice, you may need to do something else first:

Give Yourself Permission

You must be diligent and dedicated or you wouldn't be a sojourner, reading this book. You have probably been working for months or years to get overseas. You have a strong motivation to *get to work.*

Are you, perhaps, not patient with yourself? Most likely, you don't want any stress symptoms—which you may see as weakness. You'd like to get this first part of sojourning over with, feel competent—and start seeing results.

But to become healthy and effective, you will need to *give yourself permission* to do the things that manage stress: slow down, be patient with yourself, rest more, take time to exercise, add joy. If you are not sure whether God would give you such permission, consider:

> *It's useless to rise early and go to bed late, and work your worried fingers to the bone. Don't you know he enjoys giving rest to those he loves? (Psalm 127:2, The Message)*

Honestly, do you have permission to take care of yourself?

☐ **yes,** ☐ **no,** ☐ **maybe**

If you don't have permission, what might help?

_____

_____

_____

I hope you will "receive" permission to take care of yourself by managing stress because I know from years of experience that sojourners who put into practice these six tasks have better physical and mental health, stay on the field longer, have better relationships, and have more radiant lives.

So let's get practical about managing stress:

1. Get Enough Sleep!

You *know* how many hours of sleep you actually need each night although you may not want to accept the reality. It is the number of hours that gives you optimal functioning. "Enough sleep" means you wake up naturally, without an alarm. Enough sleep means you're not sleepy or grouchy during the day. Instead you are alert and engaged.

Don't think about how much sleep someone else needs or how much sleep you *wish* you needed.

How many hours of sleep do you *actually need* to function well? _____

How about accepting that reality? Are you getting that much sleep? _____

If you can't change your morning schedule to sleep longer, you'll need to go to bed earlier at night. You may need to relearn your "going to sleep rituals," if they got left behind in the move. Whatever you used to do: watch the late show, put the dog out, check the locks, turn out the lights, read a bit—your system became accustomed to those signals that meant, "Wind down, get ready for sleep." If your old cues won't work now, you need to develop new ones.

Make your bedroom as cool, comfortable, quiet, and dark as possible. It is worth the effort it takes to do so.

Research on sleep informs us that not only are body systems renewed during sleep, but emotions that occur during the day are "cleaned up," stored, and lowered in intensity. In addition, our brain is not "sleeping" while we are: it is actively storing, organizing, and linking information.[2]

> During periods of intense learning, our brain especially needs the downtime while we are sleeping to consolidate new information.

It makes sense then, that you would need more sleep in the early months of a sojourn. If you are already getting as many hours of sleep as you used to, but still feel fatigued, you may need to add an extra hour of sleep until you adjust to your new life.

Or you may need to squeeze in a twenty to thirty-minute afternoon nap. A *short* nap can be helpful, while longer naps leave you feeling groggy.

What are practical ways you can add another hour of sleep to your nights? Or a nap?

_____

_____

_____

When your computer freezes up or your smart phone stops working, what do experts say to do first? Turn it off and let it reset.

So power down. Go off-line. Let your system reset.

Sleep is God's gift for tired people who have much to learn.

2. Get a Little Exercise

Research continues to accumulate showing how much good exercise does for us: it helps our circulatory system, which helps our immune system; it removes toxins from our bodies; it helps the digestive tract get into appropriate rhythms; it creates strong bones. There's also evidence that exercise helps alleviate depression, reduce anxiety, and increase the activity of the brain—preventing dementia and decay.

So whether we enjoy exercise or not (and some of us just don't), the simple fact is that exercise helps reduce and prevent the negative effects of stress.

Therefore during this especially stressful period of your sojourn, it makes sense to recommend that you try to do a *little* exercise. *But only a little.*

Right now in your life, I am recommending exercise for stress management. Exercise, at this point, is not for getting in shape, or losing weight, although those are good goals you can work on later if you like. Right now we're talking about managing and reducing stress—only.

So start small. Don't expect great things of yourself. Just get your body moving, perspire a little, stretch those muscles, and feel a touch of physical fatigue.

Step 1: Ask yourself, of the kinds of exercise that you used to do, which of them might actually be *possible* in your new environment?

_____

_____

_____

Before my husband and I moved to the northern coast of Colombia in our mid-fifties, my husband jogged four miles every other day, and I went to a women's gym three times a week. But in Colombia, my husband found our city streets impossible to run in because of pot-holes, traffic, and crowds. Yet running outside the city was dangerous because of possible shooting or kidnapping. Eventually, he found a jogging route that snaked through certain neighborhoods and ended at a school track. If he ran very early in the morning, that worked for him.

I found the gyms in our city crowded, noisy, and hard to get to. I adapted the exercise routine I had learned, doing it in my home to my own (much preferred) selection of music. To vary the routine, I ran up and down the stairs of our five-story apartment building.

Step 2: If previous habits of exercise are just not adaptable, what new forms of exercise might you consider? Remember, for now, keep them simple!

- ☐ a short calisthenics routine in your own home?
- ☐ exercising to a video?
- ☐ walking in your neighborhood, or a nearby park?*
- ☐ swimming?

- ☐ playing team sports at a local school?
- ☐ biking?
- ☐ racquet ball or tennis?
- ☐ jogging?
- ☐ a simple stretching routine?
- ☐ other: _____

Note: if you walk while burdened with belongings, holding on to children, and/or watching for traffic or obstacles, you may work off a few calories, but that kind of walking is not reducing stress. In order to get maximum stress reduction benefit from walking, you need to be unencumbered, able to swing your arms, take long strides, breathe deeply, and enjoy your walk. Check with someone who knows the area to make sure the route you wish to walk is a safe one.

Be realistic:

What is the best time of day for you to exercise? _____

How many days a week do you plan to exercise? _____

When will you begin? _____

3. Add Activities that Refresh

Below you'll find a list of activities that some people find refreshing. If you find any of them enjoyable, put a check next to those that you *can make use of now:*

☐ creating art (painting, sculpture, etc.)	☐ journaling
☐ listening to music	☐ exploring the internet
☐ cooking	☐ playing a video game
☐ taking a bath or shower	☐ working on a puzzle
☐ watching television/movies	☐ getting out in nature
☐ working on a craft	☐ stopping for tea or coffee
☐ coloring	☐ calling (writing) a friend
☐ reading	☐ gardening

Which of these are *easy* for you to use as stress relief? Please put two checks next to those that are particularly easy to use now, in your new country.

Which of the possibilities above might require creativity in order to adapt them for use in your new country? Please circle those.

Hobbies are activities that refresh and give joy so I recommend them wholeheartedly. If you have a hobby you can easily enjoy at this point in your sojourn, by all means do so! Reading a novel, playing with photography, embroidery, knitting, crocheting, cooking, games, and puzzles are all workable—if the materials are available. But leave for later hobbies that require time and energy you may not have at present.

Now please stop and think a moment: Are there refreshing activities, small "happiness breaks," hobby-like activities not listed above, or that you have not tried before that could be stress relievers in your present situation? What are they?

_____

_____

_____

Research shows that simple pleasures slow us down, reduce blood pressure, drain away excess adrenaline, relax muscle tension, and remind us there is joy in our daily lives if we make room for it.

Note: some of the "activities that refresh" listed above involve using an electronic device. *But please exercise care! Electronic devices can be a mixed bag.* It may be refreshing to read an article online, play a video game, check social media posts, or watch a short video.

But the problem with checking an electronic device is that you can also be exposed to negative input you didn't expect. Even if you access your device to play a game or read for relaxation, it is easy to get sucked in to seeing other texts, advisories, news posts, and messages. Such unintended results may not help your stress level. Think twice about using electronic devices as a refreshing activity unless you can guarantee you'll only access what is restful.

4. Manage Connections from Home

> *"They aren't learning the language!" the supervisor of new sojourners complained. "And they aren't building relationships with people here—they're always on their phones. I'm about ready to take their phones away!"*

Taking phones away from sojourners would be an unrealistic solution. Those connections to home are a needed and important part of life. But it is true that connections from back home can create stress and need to be handled wisely by the sojourner.

Of course, in some locations, sojourners can't have smart phones or tablets; they may be fortunate to have internet access at all! In such locations, it might seem simpler to manage communication with home, but intentional management is still important. Why? Because the sojourner has a limited amount of emotional energy and brain space.

> *Brad is learning verb forms in his new language, but hears his phone buzz. He checks it: it's a message from a friend back home, in English, of course. Brad grins, answers the message, then tries to remember the verb conjugations he was practicing. It takes him more than a minute to refocus and he has less concentration.*

> *Sally connects with her sister every evening by Skype. It helps Sally feel less homesick, but it is also draining because her sister is very needy at this time. In the daytime, Sally has little energy for other relationships, saving what she has for her evening calls.*

Contrary to what many think, humans cannot multitask well: we can only give our full attention to one thing at a time—but we can quickly switch our attention from one target to another. Doing so has a cost, however: the more we shift our attention from one target to another, the more the quality of attention decreases—and brain fatigue increases.

Constantly switching attention from one language and culture to another is exhausting. Trying to maintain relationships from back home and at the same time find the courage and initiative to begin new relationships is also stressful.

How much time per day are you spending on electronic devices? _____

Are you comfortable with that amount of time and the results? _____

Please describe any instances in which responding to connections from home was distracting, stressful, or not helpful to your adjustment process?

_____

_____

_____

Somehow a new sojourner must stay appropriately connected to family, friends, and culture back home, yet manage to reserve emotional energy and concentration for tasks and relationships in the new culture.

A great solution is to *compartmentalize*. For example, a new sojourner could *limit his or her exposure* to information and connections via electronic devices in the home language to particular days of the week or particular times of day.

The sojourner should also prayerfully consider his or her priorities and decide exactly when and how much they will be connected.

Examples:

1. Turn off notification noises or pop-ups to minimize distraction.

2. Choose a specific time of day to check messages—only do so then.

3. Plan to do social media or e-mail work in English only three times per week.

4. Choose two or three specific times per week when you will be available to family or friends for contact.

   • Let friends and family know when those times are.

   • Tell them not to worry if you are not available at other times or if you don't respond immediately to messages.

   • Help them understand that although you care for them, you don't have the ability to connect as much as you or they might wish.

Making such choices will have a significant impact on the amount of stress you experience and on your progress in learning language and building relationships in your land of sojourn.

This is—again—a matter of accepting your limits, and being a good steward.

You are not a helpless responder here! You have choices.

5. Two Effective Techniques

Two coping mechanisms that studies have repeatedly shown to be effective at reducing the negative effects of stress on the body are: deep breathing and progressive relaxation training. They are easy to learn, easy to do, and worth using.

Deep Breathing:

It is simply not possible to breathe in and out deeply and rhythmically and at the same time stay tense and anxious. This is why deep breathing is taught as a stress and anxiety reducing tool.

When I worked in a large city hospital as a psychology intern, I saw patients going into the operating room who were significantly helped by learning to breathe deeply and relax.

Not only does deep breathing relax us, it also provides oxygen-starved cells with new life, and carries harmful toxins out of our system. This helps prevent the symptoms and illnesses that come from cumulative stress.

Take some time to try this reliable tool. It's easy:

Make sure the clothing around your waist or abdomen is not tight. Then take a deep, deep breath. A big one: not only up in your chest, but way down into your abdomen.

Now, let the breath out slowly. It helps slow your exhalation if you pretend you are blowing gently on hot soup. Don't hurry to breathe again: inhale when your body tells you it is necessary.

Breathe in slowly and deeply again. Breathe out slowly. Already you may feel more relaxed and less anxious. Continue to breathe in and out slowly; concentrate on breathing, and nothing else.

You have just learned and practiced the basics of deep breathing.[3]

The beauty of this simple technique is not only that it works so well, but that it can be done invisibly, anywhere, anytime. No one can tell you are managing stress.

Breathing deeply works to reduce tension and anxiety because our Creator made our bodies that way. But imagine the benefits of combining deep breathing and at the same time focusing our mind on the One who gives each breath. Breathing deeply while praying is a combination that realigns body and soul into the state we want for optimal functioning: relaxed, alert, trusting God.

Note: children can learn this simple way of reducing anxiety and tension. Suggest they pretend they are their favorite animal breathing deeply and stretching.

Progressive Relaxation

"Muscular tension is your body's way of letting you know you are under stress … when you experience stress you tense your body."[4]

When stress is short-lived, your body relaxes again, but when stress is ongoing, certain muscle groups in your body become chronically tensed.

Do a quick body scan. Now put a check next to the parts of your body where you feel an accumulation of tension.

☐ neck	☐ shoulders	☐ upper back
☐ lower back	☐ facial muscles	☐ jaw
☐ upper thighs	☐ legs	

To reduce accumulated tension such as you have just identified, Edmund Jacobson developed a technique he called progressive relaxation.[5]

The basic technique involves tensing a group of muscles, then letting that muscle group completely relax. Jacobson found that first tensing the muscles and then letting them relax is more effective than just "telling your muscles to relax." Experts suggest that tensing and relaxing the same group of muscles two times in a row is most effective.

If you find yourself carrying tension, or experiencing head, neck, shoulder, or back aches, you would profit from progressive muscle relaxation. You are welcome to look up the procedure online, or in the references provided.[6] But the technique is not difficult:

> *Lie down on a bed, on the floor, or stretch out in a comfortable chair. Make sure your clothing is not restrictive. Begin by breathing in and out slowly and deeply. Then tighten up each of the muscle groups listed below, one at a time: tighten the muscle group, then allow it to relax. Do each group twice. Begin with the muscles in your face, jaw, and neck. (E.g., "scrunch up" the muscles around your eyes, then relax. Make your jaw tense and hard, then relax.) Work your way from your head, face, and neck down through the whole body.*
>
> *Proceed with:*
>
> - *face: eyes and jaw*
> - *neck*
> - *muscles in your right arm*
> - *muscles in your left arm*
> - *chest, front, and back*
> - *lower back*
> - *abdomen*
> - *upper legs*
> - *lower legs*
> - *ankles and feet*
>
> *After you have tightened and relaxed all muscle groups twice, lie still and enjoy the feeling of relaxation and reduced tension.*

Excellent results are achieved by doing the progressive muscle relaxation procedure for just fifteen minutes per day.

Once you have begun to notice where you carry tension in your body, you can reduce cumulative tension by pausing several times a day to simply notice that your muscles are tense. Then allow them to relax and thereby avoid a build-up of tension.

6. Pace Yourself

One of the most important aspects of effective stress management is *recognizing* when your system has maxed out, and you need a break. The stress symptoms you checked above are cues you should pay attention to. They are like the "idiot light" that comes on a car's dashboard indicating low oil.

If you feel shaky, tense, nauseated, or tired, *don't* just try to keep going: that only does damage to your already exhausted system. Instead, take an hour off, take the afternoon off, or take the day off—even if it is not a weekend.

Sometimes a sojourner in the midst of so many adjustments just needs a healthy time out. A family may need to stay at home for a day in their pajamas. A single worker may need to spend the afternoon at the pool or seeing a movie.

If you fear that such actions are lazy or irresponsible—or that they might be perceived that way—pray about it. If you need to ask a supervisor's permission to take time off: ask. As you try to be sensitive to the Lord's guidance in the care of your "jar of clay," you will develop greater ability to use your common sense, hear His voice, and feel confident about when it is good stewardship to take a break.

Be wise and proactive in regard to pacing. Look ahead and anticipate time periods that will be tiring, tense, or stressful. Plan extra rest *before* those times come up. Try to have "nothing to do" the evening or the day after an intense or draining activity.

If you have several consecutive days of stressful activity coming up, schedule at least one day off afterward, and subsequent days with lighter responsibilities. Don't expect to just go back to the grind and catch up on everything you missed. That's a recipe for burnout.

If you need to, if you can, and if it helps—get away. (Sometimes getting away sounds good, but it can be more trouble than it's worth. You decide.)

Pacing involves two important skills:

1. Recognizing when you are stressed and taking the downtime you need.
2. Looking ahead and realistically estimating how much intensity, busyness, or stress you can handle well. Use rest, exercise, and refreshing activities *before* they are needed to prevent stress. That's good stewardship.

Look ahead at your next week and month. Are there times of intensity or stress ahead? If so, how can you preventively pace yourself by planning times for rest in advance and time for recovery after?

_____

_____

_____

_____

Jarring

We are only issued one jar. One body. For a lifetime.

I'm sure you expect your jar of clay to serve you, and God, for a while yet.

If so: rest—enough. Exercise—a little. Breathe deeply—often. Relax those muscles—regularly. Seek out small (or large) doses of refreshing activities. Manage electronic connections. Pace yourself with wisdom.

Meditate on God's goodness and care as you do these things. Seek His guidance as you manage your jar. It's *His* jar, really. He wants you to honor it, not abuse it: for His sake.

Give your jar a break! It has been through a lot recently.

Additional references for devotional study

Psalm 16   2 Corinthians 4:1-18
Psalm 23   Philippians 1:20
1 Corinthians 6:12, 19-20

Footnotes

1. *Getting Well Again.* O Carl Simonton; Stephanie Matthews-Simonton; James L. Creighton. Bantam Books, 1978. Pages 46-55.

2. *The Sleep Revolution: Transforming Your Life, One Night at a Time.* Arianna Huffington. Harmony Books, 2016.

3. *The Relaxation and Stress Reduction Workbook.* Martha Davis, Elizabeth Eshelman, Matthew McKay. New Harbinger Publications. 1982.

4. Ibid. page 17.

5. Ibid. Pages 23-27.

6. Ibid.

Bibliography

Davis, Martha; Eshelman, Elizabeth Robbins; McKay, Matthew. *The Relaxation and Stress Reduction Workbook.* New Harbinger Publications. 2008.

Hart, Archibald. *Adrenaline and Stress.* Word Publishing. 1995

Huffington, Arianna. *The Sleep Revolution: Transforming Your Life, One Night at a Time.* Harmony Books, 2016.

Simonton, O. Carl; Simonton, Stephanie Matthews; Creighton, James L. *Getting Well Again.* Bantam Books. 1978

chapter 3

Raspberry Jam: Grieving Insignificant—and Significant Losses

Mourning our losses allows us to let go. Only then do we have the emotional space to open ourselves to new people, new experiences—and joy.

When we lived in Honduras, someone brought me a jar of greatly longed for and coveted raspberry jam. There may be wild raspberries of some kind in Honduras, but, at least then, there was no such thing as raspberry jam, and I loved the stuff and missed it. I hoarded that jam, carefully eking out a teaspoon at a time so it would last as long as possible. A house guest unwittingly helped themselves to nearly a third of the jar one day when I was not around, and when I discovered it, I was speechless at the effrontery of the guest and at my own sense of outraged loss.

Fortunately for us both, the guest was not present when I made this discovery. "It's only raspberry jam!" I reminded myself, and eventually was able to forgive the thoughtless thief, and even laugh.

I T CAN CATCH US BY SURPRISE—that sudden lump in the throat, the anger, or stinging behind the eyes that happens when our "small loss quota" has been reached after a major move into a new culture. Because, we're funny. It isn't one loss that does it: missing Mother's Day, say, or not going out to lunch with a friend. It's not the next loss either: not being able to see the Super Bowl, or attend a professional conference, or find our favorite kind of restaurant.

It's not any *one* thing, really. It's all those things mentioned, plus not feeling like we know where we're going and what we're doing and who we are.

And then the raspberry jam (or whatever the loss may be) becomes the straw that makes the camel get tears in his eyes. And we wonder: *What is the matter with me?*

Nothing. Nothing at all that a little grieving won't fix.

Grieving? Over raspberry jam? You've got to be kidding!

Nope. Grieving will help, but the issue isn't necessarily raspberry jam—or any other particular loss.

The fact is: Whenever we move, and especially when we move to a foreign culture, we end up with an accumulation of small and large losses. We do need to mourn them or not doing so will cause emotional and spiritual blockage.

Let's look at the "whether it's unspiritual to mourn" issue later, and right now take a look at just how many losses you have accumulated in the past few months.

Looking at Losses:

First, are there things you don't miss?

Maybe, in all the recent change you haven't realized it, but probably there are things you *don't miss!* You may feel relief as you realize you don't have to cope with certain people or problems anymore. That's okay. There are upsides to leaving a place!

What are the things, people, roles, responsibilities, or relationships you *don't* **miss?**

_____

_____

_____

Loss Can Be Confusing:

If people or things are only temporarily unavailable, are they still losses? For example, a sojourner might really miss her sister who is back home, but since the sister hasn't died, the sojourner is in frequent contact with her by e-mail and Skype, and they are likely to be together again someday, is the sister's absence a loss? Yes! Since in the present, the sojourner cannot enjoy her sister's company *as she used to or would like to*, her experience of missing that sister is a loss.

Loss can be defined as the permanent or temporary removal of an important person, object, or experience. The failure to achieve a goal or the awareness of lacking something are also losses.

What Are Your Losses, Then? What Do You Miss?

People (individual relationships):

_____

_____

_____

People (group relationships):

_____

_____

_____

Roles (formal, professional, informal):

_____

_____

_____

Places (favorite restaurants, shops, haunts, parks, church):

_____

_____

_____

Things (material objects, items, possessions, e.g. home, bed, T.V.; or elements available in a particular place or culture, like music, foods, or sports):

_____

_____

_____

Events:

_____

_____

_____

Other losses occur in moving or cross-cultural adjustment that are hard to get a handle on, but are there nonetheless. Please check those that are relevant to you:

☐ loss of familiarity   ☐ not feeling in control

☐ not feeling known   ☐ not feeling competent

☐ stripped of identity   ☐ not feeling needed

☐ not knowing whom to turn to   ☐ feeling left out

☐ no sense of belonging   ☐ feeling inadequate

☐ little recreational choice   ☐ few potential friends

☐ others? _____

Please take a moment to put your real feelings into words:

_____

_____

_____

What's the Grand Total?

Now take a moment to look over all the questions you answered above. If you have listed all your losses, this list represents _your_ cumulative total of losses piled up over past months. They probably accrued gradually, so you didn't realize the full weight of them at any one time. In a way, the cumulative effect of such losses is not quantifiable.

It isn't possible to come up with a numerical sum that conveys the full impact of many small and large losses adding up over a comparatively short period of time.

There may be days you don't think about the losses; you focus on your current life and that's enough to handle. After all, you expected to make sacrifices. But there may be other times when you experience that sudden pang that brings a lump to the throat, tears to the eyes, or just a staggering sense of absence. The loss can be a seemingly small, inconsequential something—like raspberry jam. Or the loss might be large. Or you might just feel a pervasive, sad heaviness.

Well, that's normal.

A simple, inexorable truth is that if we mourn our losses—small or large, temporary or permanent, noticeable to others or not, the acuteness of the sense of loss will eventually pass. We may still miss whatever it is, but the pain becomes less.

If you grieve for the losses listed above, sadness will lessen in time so you can be productive and joyful. But repressing or ignoring the feelings can lead to depression, irritability, or bitterness. Not paying attention to our cumulative losses allows a residue to build up inside us that gradually erodes our sense of well-being, our spontaneity, our joy.

Is Grieving Unspiritual?

"Foxes have holes and birds of the air have nests, but the Son of Man has no place to lay his head," Jesus said (Matthew 8:20, NIV). There is a poignancy to this statement that implies Jesus missed having a place of His own. Clearly, He did stop and rest, but He didn't have a resting place that was His earthly *home.*

It does not say in this passage that Jesus was mourning. In fact, His words are spoken to a potential follower, and contain an implicit warning: "Following me involves cost; there are losses—like not having a home." Like not feeling at home.

But also implicit in Jesus' words is *recognition* of the losses: they are not ignored. They are counted and absorbed.

Essentially, mourning losses accrued in crossing cultures for the sake of Jesus' kingdom is the absorption of the cost of discipleship.

Mourning allows us to recognize a loss for what it costs us, admit its impact, absorb the pain—and let it go.

We need to *let go* so that we can go on undistracted by a lingering sense of deprivation, guilt, or resentment. Grieving helps us do so.

Jesus, "Man of Sorrows"

I am so thankful that Jesus was "a man of sorrows and acquainted with grief" and "familiar with suffering" (Isaiah 53:3, KJV). "Surely, he took up our infirmities and carried our sorrows," wrote the prophet Isaiah, "and by his wounds we are healed" (Isaiah 53:4a, 5, NIV).

Jesus knows all about it. He lived in a Mediterranean country dominated by oppressive Roman rule and a fiercely legalistic religion. There were no antibiotics, no immunizations. Surely Jesus saw friends and relatives sicken, suffer, and die. He saw people abused and mistreated. Probably He lost Joseph, His earthly father, in His youth, since Jesus' siblings and Mary are mentioned in the gospels, but Joseph is not.

Jesus' own brothers despised and disowned him. He never had a wife or children or a home. All around Him He consistently saw rigid hearts and lack of faith. His disciples persistently misunderstood Him—and one betrayed Him. Jesus was familiar with loss and disappointment—He knew them intimately like old friends.

> *When Jesus was told of the brutal murder of His cousin and colleague in ministry John the Baptist, He "withdrew by boat privately to a solitary place." He also wept openly over the fate of Jerusalem. And approaching the grave of His friend Lazarus, He was "deeply moved" and wept so obviously that bystanders commented on His emotion.*
>
> *In the garden of Gethsemane, Jesus experienced such depth of emotion that it produced a physical reaction like sweating drops of blood (Matthew 14:13, Luke 19:28-44, John 11, Hebrews 5:7-9).*
>
> *Note: If you would profit from more in-depth study of how Jesus expressed emotion and mourned, please see the study guide at the end of this chapter. It includes references and helpful questions.*

Jesus, God incarnate, modeled a life that acknowledged loss and pain—but persevered toward His goal anyway.

Here's the thing: It doesn't matter what size the loss is—if it gets to us, if we feel it, then we need to mourn it and let go.

The God of the Bible is not a stoic God afraid to express emotion: passage after passage in the prophets, the Psalms, and the New Testament shows a God who expresses outrage, sadness, loss, and grief. (See "Additional Bible Study Aids" at the end of the chapter.)

Nor does God have a problem with *us* experiencing or expressing emotions related to loss or grief. The problem occurs when we get stuck in negative emotions.

"But Jesus was dealing with *huge* losses," you might protest, "and so have others, the heroes and martyrs of the faith, the persecuted church—my losses are so small! Shouldn't I 'just get over it'?"

Here's the thing: It doesn't matter what size the loss is—if it gets to us, if we feel it, then we need to mourn it and let go.

Paradoxically, engaging in the grieving we need to do allows us to embrace being a living sacrifice. Grieving helps us accept our losses so that we can be a sacrifice that goes on living without being weighed down by unshed tears.

Mourning Is a Skill We Can Learn

Mourning is primarily a *reflective* process. People may think of grieving as crying or experiencing overwhelming sadness. Certainly grieving may include tears, or overwhelming emotion, but it doesn't always and it doesn't have to. What it *does* require is thought and prayer: the kind of thought and prayer that is usually best done in solitude.

If you don't do well trying to reflect on your own or if you are an external or verbal processor, you might prefer to find a trusted listener to whom you can reflect out loud.

This trusted listener needs to be someone who won't question your faith or your commitment as you mourn, but who will accept your grief and understand it as part of your adjustment process. The person might be a friend from back home, or someone who is going through (or has gone through) cross-cultural adjustment and who will therefore understand.

Whether you seek out solitude, a trusted companion, or both, make time for the thoughtfulness and reflection you need.

The Tasks of Good Mourning:

1. Find or make time alone.

Alone can mean home alone; in your bedroom alone; in a library, church, or park; or just walking by yourself. What you need, whether you prefer solitude or privacy with a friend, is uninterrupted time—time set apart for a valuable process.

2. Identify the losses.

Name the losses to yourself, to your friend, to God, or on paper. Zero in on what hurts, even if you think it is silly or trivial. Try to identify just what it is about that person or thing that you miss, e.g., admitting you miss playing basketball with your friends might reveal that you miss not only the exercise, but the jokes and laughter, the presence of a particular person, or the status of being part of that group.

3. Name and feel the feelings.

Go ahead, *name* them: "I feel so sad." "I feel deprived and angry." "I feel lonely, lethargic, depressed, stupid, resentful …" "And I feel guilty for feeling these things!"

As we name the losses, dig into them, and recognize them, tears can well up. Sobs may come. For others, no tears are involved, just a hard thinking process, a feeling of honest recognition, followed by relief.

(If you find that in opening up your feelings, you are unable to stop weeping or you become depressed, you are probably the victim of spillover mourning: mourning that is related to past losses or past abuse. If this happens, please seek professional help.)

4. Pray throughout

Mourning is fundamentally a spiritual process because our bottom-level issue is with God. We hold our pain against Him.

After all, He is sovereign, right? He *could* give us anything; He *could* help us not feel these deep feelings of loss and pain. The truth is: He could. Therefore we must bring our feelings out in His presence and address them *to Him*. No use trying to admit the feelings to ourselves, fix it all, and *then* go to Him.

Usually, as we open up our pain (and perhaps anger) in His presence, we begin to accept the hurt and loss as part of what He is asking of us. When we do this, the pain doesn't go away, but it becomes lighter, more bearable. We learn that *this loss* is part of His assignment for us right now, and it comes with His strength attached, if we accept it. He may not take the pain away, but He is *with us* in bearing it.

Mourning is fundamentally a spiritual process because our bottom-level issue is with God. We hold our pain against Him.

A few more tips

1. The onion operation

Sometimes we have to mourn the same thing or person more than once. I call this the onion operation. That's normal. When we first become aware of a loss, we do as much mourning as we can. And we go on. But sometimes we need to peel away another layer, perhaps cry, or reflect a little more.

2. The straw on the camel's back factor

It is not always the large losses that get to us. Each of us has a cumulative effect level. When we collect enough losses—little or big—we start to feel the heaviness that means we need to grieve.

Keep an eye on the loss factor: Don't dismiss something that bothers you as negligible or stupid. It might be just a straw, but since you want your camel to function and not break down in the desert, you know what to do.

Keep an eye on the loss factor: Don't dismiss something that bothers you as negligible or stupid.

---

3. Styles of mourning differ greatly

How we mourn differs from culture to culture, and from person to person. Some hide their grief behind a stoic façade and need solitude to deal with feelings. Others bawl unashamedly in public. Some shed tears; others never do. Some need to talk; others would rather not talk at all.

Some people are anticipatory mourners—they cry two, three, four months before the loss occurs. This exasperates the mate or parent who only mourns after the loss. Some individuals mourn right as they lose something. And some of us do all three: anticipatory, in situ, and post-loss mourning.

There is nothing wrong with any of these styles. One is not better than the other, and we usually don't get to choose our style: we just come that way. But we do need to work at being patient with each other—especially our spouse, child, or roommate. We need to recognize their style as legitimate and important—as long as the mourning gets done.

Conclusions

Living sacrifices must grieve losses. (Dead sacrifices, of course, don't have to.)

Ah, so unpopular, this mourning business. We all avoid it like the plague—myself included. But I have learned from God's Word, from my own experience in crossing cultures, and from working with hundreds of sojourners how important this task of doing the mourning is.

In going to a country and culture not familiar to you for the sake of the Gospel, you committed yourself to being a living sacrifice. You knew it would be hard. But you may not have known just which sacrifices would hurt the most, or how bad that hurt would be. How could you have known, until you were *actually experiencing the losses?*

So now comes the time to actually *make the sacrifice. Live it.*

Please list below the losses that have surprised you—either in that they are losses at all, or in how much they sometimes hurt:

_____

_____

Please list the losses you think you have noticed, paid attention to, and begun to appropriately mourn:

_____

_____

_____

Now please name losses you have not yet fully paid attention to or done the mourning for:

_____

_____

_____

How can you make time and space to do the mourning you need to do?

_____

_____

_____

Paradoxically, engaging in the grieving we need to do allows us to embrace being a living sacrifice. Grieving helps us accept our losses so that we can be a sacrifice that goes on living without being weighed down by unshed tears. Because mourning allows us to let go. Then, and only then, do we have the emotional space to open ourselves to new people, new experiences—and joy.

So have at it.

Mourning our losses is not a negation of our commitment: it is part of actualizing that commitment.

> _We don't have a priest who is out of touch with our reality. He's been through_
> _weakness and testing, experienced it all—all but the sin. So let's walk right_
> _up to him and get what he is so ready to give. Take the mercy, accept the help._
> _—Hebrews 4:15-16, The Message_

Bible References for Additional Study

Psalm 16	Lamentations 3:1-58	2 Corinthians 1:3-4, 8, 9
Psalm 31:9	Hosea 11	2 Corinthians 4:7-18
Psalm 56:8	Matthew 5:4	Philippians 2:5-11
Psalm 119:75	Matthew 8:20	Philippians 3:7-11
Psalm 147:3-4	Mark 14:34	1 Timothy 4:13
Ecclesiastes 3:1, 4	Luke 19:41; Luke 22:42	Hebrews 12:2
Isaiah 53	John 11	Hebrews 4:15-16

Bibliography

Recovering from the Losses of Life. H. Norman Wright. Fleming H. Revell, Baker Book House, Grand Rapids, 1993.

The Grief Recovery Handbook: A Step-by-Step Program for Moving Beyond Loss. John W. James and Frank Cherry. Harper Perennial. 1998.

Life Is Goodbye: Life Is Hello: Grieving Well Through All Kinds of Loss. Alla Renee Bozarth, Ph.D., Hazelden, 1986.

Shattered Dreams: God's Unexpected Pathway to Joy. Larry Crabb. WaterBrook Press, 2001.

Also: check "Grief Share" and the Grief Recovery Books at *www.parable.com*

Books for Children (and Adults):

Tear Soup: A Recipe for Healing after Loss. Pat Schwiebert and Chuck DeKlyen, Illustrated by Taylor Bills. Grief Watch, Portland, OR. 2001.

Helping Children Grieve: When Someone They Love Dies. Theresa Huntley. Augsberg Fortress. 1991.

Feelings: From Sadness to Happiness. Gemser Publications S. L., 2000. Barron's Educational Series, Inc. *www.barronseduc.com*

Let's Talk about Feeling Sad. Joy Berry. Scholastic, Inc. 1996

Alexander, Who's Not (Do You Hear Me? I Mean It!) Going to Move. Judith Viorst. Aladdin Paperbacks. 1995

Study: Jesus' Expression of Emotion and Grief

To help you grapple with how Jesus dealt with His emotions, read each passage, and then answer the questions for each passage.

The passages:

1. Matthew 14:13
2. Luke 19:28-44
3. John 11
4. Hebrews 5:7-9

The questions:

What caused Jesus' expression of emotion?

_____

_____

_____

If Jesus was grieving over something, what do you think He was grieving?

_____

_____

_____

How did Jesus show His emotion?

_____

_____

_____

What do we learn about our own feelings and expression of grief from Jesus's example?

_____

_____

_____

chapter 4

Don't Sacrifice Everything: Crafting a Lifestyle that Endures

When Kent and Lisa arrived in Costa Rica to study Spanish, they felt delighted, and relieved: They had made it! How fascinating all the new sights, sounds, smells, and tastes were!

But soon the novelty wore off and they found themselves reluctant to leave the house: it was so much work to walk everywhere, or take the bus, facing crowds of strangers. They understood little Spanish, so after the first few sentences of any conversation, they felt awkward and useless. In meetings where people spoke Spanish, their attention spans lasted only ten minutes and then they felt a strange combination of boredom and anxiety. Any outing was draining; there were so many stimuli to absorb and sort through. It was much, much easier to just stay home.

IT IS COMMON FOR SOJOURNERS early in their sojourn to be tempted to just stay home. Or, even if they become restless and bored at home, they might not be sure how to get out and have fun—or if it is okay to seek out fun and fulfillment.

The temptation to stay home or the doubts about how to get fun back into life are partly due to the stress discussed in Chapter 2, and the losses described in Chapter 3. But there is more to it than stress and grief.

The apathy and low energy of early sojournerhood also happen because of the *absence of things that used to make life happy.* The absence of warm, good feelings creates a sense of emptiness. Life can be perceived as a lot of work and not much fun.

When a person experiences a series of losses, he or she feels deprived, punished. That's natural. It is how we feel when good things are taken away from us. In the case of sojourning, things weren't taken away—they were left behind. But the result is the same: we feel empty and punished.

What can be done?

Certainly, stress needs to be managed, and grieving must be done, but that is not all.

If we lose a dear friend or loved one, we not only have to survive the shock of loss and do our grieving; we also have to go out and engage in activities by ourselves—*without our friend or loved one.* This requires courage and initiative.

In the same way a sojourner must find the courage to explore activities in the new land, where things are threatening and unfamiliar.

In the next few pages, we will look at reasons why being proactive about exploring new activities isn't easy. And we'll review tips for how to craft a lifestyle that lasts by adding in appropriate recreation and fun.

In the same way a sojourner must find the courage to explore activities in the new land, where things are threatening and unfamiliar.

It Doesn't Just Happen!

Back home you probably did not think much about what made life rewarding. You simply grew up enjoying fishing because you started doing it with your grandad when you were five. Your family went to sports events or dog shows, so that's what you did. Friends played tennis, were in a band, or watched a certain television show; you were invited to join in and it was fun. Hobbies and recreation became part of your life naturally because they came with your background, your environment, and your relationships. They happened and were good gifts.

While discovering new fun activities might *just happen* in your new country, depending on serendipity to help you craft a new lifestyle could take a long, long time.

And many new sojourners, tired from stress and loss, don't feel like seeking out new activities and relationships. Except for extroverted and adventurous personality types, sojourners are understandably inclined to conserve energy and avoid risk. Being proactive may not come naturally.

But the problem with not trying new things is that the deprived, punished feeling doesn't go away.

Have you found yourself wanting to stay home, or otherwise avoid trying new experiences? If so, when and how?

Such a reaction is understandable.

But gathering your courage to try new things is essential for future well-being and effectiveness.

More than Stress Management

Previously, I have encouraged you to sometimes stay home and rest as a way to manage stress, but not *all the time*. Constantly avoiding new experiences is not a workable lifestyle. And unfortunately, merely managing stress will not get rid of that empty void.

I also encouraged you, in Chapter 2, to reduce stress by engaging in both old and new pleasurable activities that didn't take much time or effort. I hope you have found doing so helpful.

Now I want to encourage you to continue the easy-to-do fun activities, but also to consider those that take more set-up time and effort. You might have to expend time and energy gathering craft items, searching for a bicycle, or buying a kayak or a sewing machine. You may have to explore your city or surroundings for what you need. You may need to spend money.

What Do I Mean by Recreation?

Anything that is not, by your definition, *work*!

Going to restaurants, visiting parks, seeing a movie, games, hobbies, reading that is not required—those are recreation. Hiking, swimming, biking, and playing soccer qualify as exercise—but also may be done for fun. Going to museums, concerts, lectures, doing crossword puzzles, collecting coins or stamps—all can be good for you as refreshing, relaxing, educational activities.

Recreation is any activity that distracts you, refreshes you, renews you, is different from your daily grind, and isn't bad for you.

What restaurants have you gone to in the past month? What movies have you seen? What walks have you taken? What parties or concerts have you been to? What have you done for fun?

_____

_____

_____

_____

Since such activities are good for us when used in healthy and balanced ways, I believe they are God's gifts to us. That is the first reason any of us, sojourner or not, should include exercise and play in our lives. They are gifts from our loving Father.

> _"Every good and perfect gift is from above, coming down from the Father of the heavenly lights, who does not change..." (James 1:17, NIV)._

Yes, you moved overseas to serve Him, and to serve sacrificially. But while it may feel spiritual to make sacrifices, it is not wise to sacrifice more than is necessary. There's enough sacrifice already built in, in my opinion.

God doesn't change, so if He gave you good gifts in your old life, why wouldn't He do so in your new life?

It is not selfish or unspiritual to try to see which of God's good gifts in a past life can be rediscovered in a new life. And it is not selfishness, but good stewardship, to look for new gifts the Lord may provide.

God doesn't change, so if He gave you good gifts in your old life, why wouldn't He do so in your new life?

Benefits of Recreation

I encouraged you (in Chapter 2) to get enough sleep, to exercise, and to engage in activities that give joy—because all those things reduce stress. If your stress has been reduced—good!

Please continue to do what reduces stress—and here are more reasons to engage in even more recreation:

1. Sojourners who creatively engage in recreation on a regular basis move past the negative, punitive feeling that life isn't fun. Instead, they begin to experience their new home as a place with potential for joy.

2. People who make time in their lives for exercise and recreational activities tend to be physically and mentally healthier. This is a well-documented fact.

3. The more times a sojourner ventures out into his or her community for a walk, a run, or a shopping expedition, the more he or she will discover that it is safe to do so. The route, the experience, and the people gradually become familiar. Invisible dynamics of the culture begin to be recognized. After a while, greetings become commonplace, shopkeepers or passersby strike up acquaintance, relationships begin, and friendships are born.

Nicolo was a native of the island where we hosted a training program for new sojourners. He had worked with new arrivals for years. At an end of semester picnic, he and I sat on a picnic table, waiting for the volleyball game to be over. I knew I was about to be regaled with his perspective on how the semester's graduates were going to do in the future.

"That one," he said, pointing with his chin, "he is going to do great."

"Who, Jared?" I asked. "But he is still struggling with the language."

"True," Nicolo admitted. "But he plays soccer with us. He jokes. He likes our music. He has fun, and he likes us, so we like him. If he doesn't get better at language, he will be forgiven."

"That one," he pointed with his chin again, at Seth. "Not so good."

"But he's good at the language," I protested, "and he's trying hard."

"He tries hard," Nicolo admitted, "but he doesn't like it here. He always compares here to back home. He is always on the computer."

Sarah slid by, trying to spike a ball. "What about Sarah?" I asked, because I thought of her as quiet and shy.

"Oh, Sarah. She is good," affirmed Nicolo.

"Why?" I persisted.

"Because, did you know on Sundays she plays guitar at the orphanage? And on other days she is giving three kids guitar lessons and helps with crafts. So I think she will be fine."

The volleyball game ended at that point, but later I pondered Nicolo's observations. I found his criteria for success intriguing. He seemed to think that if new sojourners knew how to have fun and recreate with the local populace, they would settle in and thrive. Only time will tell if Nicolo is right, but his observations are worth keeping in mind.

4. Recreations can lead to platforms for business or ministry.

Sojourner friends in Asia loved scuba diving, and taught their children to dive. It must have been expensive, but they made the investment. As a result, crucial bonding with their children and love of the foreign country occurred while scuba diving. The kids invited friends; the parents invited friends. Scuba diving became not only fun, but a way to deepen existing relationships and create new ones. Today, the children are grown and gone, but the parents remain in the foreign country. Their scuba diving hobby has become a small business, providing them an ever-widening circle of influence.

Two women sojourners, in different countries, cooked for their families and their cooking generated curiosity among women in their host culture. Soon, one of them was giving cooking lessons, then a cooking class with Bible study.

The other started decorating cakes for special events—then was asked to teach others to decorate as well, providing multiple opportunities for relationships and sharing. Who knew the joy of cooking could evolve into ministry?

Which of the four benefits above is most meaningful or motivating for you?

_____

_____

_____

Of the hobbies or recreations you already do in your country of sojourn, which ones would you like to increase, or expand?

_____

_____

_____

Obstacles to Reckon With

My friend was doing her best to come up with activities she used to enjoy that might lower her symptoms of depression. "I love to swim," she confessed, "and sit in the sun afterward."

"Well, couldn't you do that?" I asked. "There are clubs in your city that have swimming pools. Could you join one?"

"But they're so expensive!" she protested.

"How much?" I asked.

She told me. For someone with her income, it was pricey, but possible.

"Hmmm," I said, "how much has it cost you in medical appointments and medications to deal with this depression?"

Her eyes opened very wide.

"Wouldn't a yearly fee at the swimming club be worth it if you weren't depressed anymore?" I persisted.

"I hadn't thought of it like that!" she admitted.

1. Costs

"I can't afford it" is the reason I hear most often for why sojourners don't have fun. Sometimes it is true: the cost of a recreation *can be* so exorbitant, it is truly out of the question.

Perhaps what we can't afford as a luxury, we can afford as an investment in long-term health and effectiveness.

In other cases, the cost of a recreation is a matter of priorities: a sojourner may think of a recreation as out of the question because it costs more than it did back home. But "more" is a relative value. The recreation may cost more than back home, but other things in the country of sojourn may cost less. Or the recreation may seem expensive, but once the initial outlay is paid, ongoing costs might not be prohibitive.

It is worth considering whether the cost of fun might be worth the benefits.

Perhaps what we can't afford as a luxury, we can afford as an investment in long-term health and effectiveness.

2. Host culture opinion

"My host country people won't understand it" is another objection given for why a recreation shouldn't be pursued. Again, sometimes this is true, and creating cross-cultural misunderstanding is not advisable. But think long and hard. It could be that the way a recreation is presented, or engaged in, could make it into a plus instead of a minus.

> *When my husband and I moved to the northern coast of Colombia, a place fraught with civil war and drug cartels, there were few safe recreations for the likes of us. We tried to join a club with tennis courts, a pool, and a track, but were denied. Then we tried a golf club. We didn't have to join, and my husband enjoyed golf while I enjoyed the view. At first we worried that our Colombian friends would think our recreation extravagant, but they didn't seem to. Perhaps they viewed it as one more eccentricity of an eccentric couple! Also, they cared about our safety and were glad we found a safe recreation.*

> *Occasionally, we invited Colombian co-workers as guests for the day. They learned about golf, we got to know them better, and they began to mention seeing golf in the news.*

> *For us, the trip on country roads, the wide open green spaces, and just being away from work refreshed us so we could go back to the heat, dirt, and danger of daily life—and survive our years there without burnout.*

While a sojourner's engagement in recreational pursuits *might be seen as negative* by host country colleagues, in other cases the sojourner's activity creates positive relationships and can blossom into ministry. Don't assume your host country colleagues will view a recreation as bad. Seek wise counsel. And pray about it.

3. What will friends back home think?

"Our friends back home won't understand" is another reason given by sojourners for not engaging in a recreation. Underlying the statement is a fear of disapproval.

If friends back home are aware of the sojourner's recreational choices, some may approve, others may not care, and some—not having an informed perspective on the stress that accrues in sojourning—may not understand why the expenditure of time or money in recreation is warranted.

If someone from back home is aware of the sojourner's recreations, or is likely to visit and participate in the recreation, then some explanation of the sacrifices that affect the sojourner and the importance of the recreation for good health and adjustment can be offered.

Often, the sojourner's fears about what people back home might disapprove of are exaggerated, and they find, instead, that friends back home are thankful when the sojourner finds activities that help them adjust.

4. My colleagues never play!

"I never see my colleagues engage in recreation; they only work." Whether the statement refers to expat or host country colleagues, the implication is that if the new sojourner plays, they will be seen as slackers. Sadly, this sometimes happens.

However, appearances can be deceptive: it may look to the sojourner as if colleagues never play, but more in-depth knowledge of the colleagues in question may reveal that they make time for things they enjoy that the sojourner either would not enjoy or is not aware of.

In our early years in countries of the Caribbean, I was concerned for our pastoral colleagues, who worked long hours and didn't seem to take time off. Gradually, however, I realized that although these colleagues did indeed work hard, they worked differently than their North American counterparts. Perhaps they didn't take a day off, but they freely mixed business with pleasure: a pastoral visit spilled over into watching a football match; a walk across a campus became an impromptu soccer game; an errand evolved into discussion of local gossip, politics, and jokes. The pastors did do trips to the beach, but those trips included members of the youth group and stops along the way to see friends or pick up supplies. I learned that these pastors did work hard, and they did play. They just wove their play into their work and their work into their play. This would not have worked for me, but it seemed to work for them.

Despite my discoveries in the Caribbean, there are places where expatriate or host country colleagues of new sojourners don't engage in recreation in healthy ways, and put pressure on new arrivals to follow the same workaholic patterns they do. In such cases, what can the new sojourner do?

The new sojourner could attempt to explain why he or she chooses to engage in recreation and seek to educate by word and example. Such attempts to educate might succeed—or create friction. It is possible that a new sojourner may need to conform to the prevailing values for a period, and hope for the right time to instigate change and embrace recreation for health. In situations where colleagues or teammates have differing opinions about the value of recreation and time off, I suggest a great deal of prayer, and requests for guidance from wise supervisors, counselors, and mentors.

Of the obstacles to recreation listed below, which ones most affect you? Put a check by the objections that apply to you. Or write other concerns you have:

- ☐ It's too much trouble
- ☐ I don't have the energy
- ☐ My expat or host country colleagues don't play
- ☐ Friends back home won't understand
- ☐ Host country people may criticize or not understand
- ☐ It costs too much money
- ☐ Other: _____

Of the recreations you used to engage in back home, but haven't tried in your country of sojourn, which ones have you concluded are simply not possible or advisable to try? Why?

_____

_____

_____

A Helpful Mind-set

Before you think further about recreations that might work for you, I'd like to review a mental perspective that is helpful when you try out a recreation in a new place:

1. If you have doubts about the value of looking for recreation in your new land, view such an investment as part of your assignment. If your current assignment is to adjust to your new country, then exploring potential recreation is an integral part of that assignment—not something extracurricular.

2. View yourself as an amateur anthropologist. If you have a spouse, children, or teammates along for the ride, encourage that perspective in them as well. Anthropologists study cultures by watching behaviors and interactions and trying to understand them. They aren't judgmental. They don't try to change the culture; they just try to understand what is happening. As a newbie in the country, lower your own anxiety by viewing each outing as an opportunity to watch and learn. Instead of thinking you are supposed to like everything, or instead of reacting to something as annoying or disgusting, bring your curiosity to the experience and ponder. Bring your sense of humor, too.

3. View any first-time foray of exploration as an experiment. It may succeed—or fail. The value of an experiment is in the learning. If you go out with your friend or family to try a new restaurant, don't say, "This will be fun!" Instead say, "This is an experiment. It may be fun, or we might not like it. Either way, we'll learn. If it's a good experience, we'll go again. If it's terrible, we'll know not to go there." After all, even back home you didn't always enjoy every restaurant or park you tried. Why would you expect to do so in your new home?

4. Debrief after the event. After the excursion, it is a good idea to review what happened. Ask yourself, and other participants, "What was good? What was fun? What was not so great? Would we want to do this again? If so, what might we do differently?"

Also ask, "What did I learn about the people? The language? The customs? The geography? What valuable inferences can I make? Whom can I ask about what I didn't understand? Or what I think I learned?"

Finally, ask, "What did I learn about myself?"

"My kids don't want to leave the house!" Amanda confessed.

"And actually, neither do I. If we're out in public, people mob us and pinch my kids because they're not used to white-skinned people. I don't know how to help my kids."

"Ease all of you into it," I suggested. "Do a short, planned excursion every other day, and tell your kids how long it will be. Have a treat and a discussion when you get home.

"Ask your kids what they didn't like, and what they did. Sympathize. Ask them what they learned. Foster their natural curiosity. Help them see each experience as a mixture of good, bad, and interesting. Right now they are focusing only on what they don't like.

"Talk about how each of you could respond to being crowded and pinched. Discuss funny, unacceptable ways of responding, and good ways to respond. Make it a game.

"Also, let them know parts of this are hard for you, too. Remind them that such feelings are natural. Explain what helps you choose to continue even when some things are hard."

Now that you have the right mental approach, you're ready for more questions about potential recreations.

Of the hobbies and recreations you used to do back home, which ones have you *not yet* tried in your country of sojourn, but with effort, time, or expense, you can imagine they might be possible to enjoy now?

_____

_____

_____

Introverts/Extroverts and Recreation

Should you do your hobbies and recreations by yourself? Or with others?

Yes.

Obviously, some hobbies are usually done in solitude—such as reading. Others, such as team sports, only happen in a group. But apart from the requirements of the activity itself, you will need to consider *what you need at any given time.*

Some of us are introverts. We genuinely need time alone to recover from the stimulation and intensity of life. If you have introverted tendencies, you may well seek out recreations that feed your need for quiet and solitude. That is fine: the need for solitude is a genuine one. But introverts also need refreshing ways to be with other people. So, even if you enjoy one or two of your recreations alone, plan other recreations that involve others.

If all of your current recreations tend to be solitary, discover others that involve you outside of your house, and with other people.

Extroverts—who enjoy being around people, and need to interact with people in order to feel whole—need to ask themselves similar questions. Generally, extroverts prefer recreations that involve human interaction. But extroverts need a certain amount of solitude as well. In fact, in the middle of much stress and stimulation, extroverts (and introverts!) may need more solitude than usual.

Introvert, extrovert, or anywhere in between: pay attention to what you need. Organize your hobbies and recreations so that you have more than one, or more than one way to enjoy them, so you can accommodate your need—at any given time—for solitude or interaction.

Which of your current recreations are meeting your present needs for solitude or escape?

_____

_____

_____

Which current recreations are meeting your need to be around, or interacting with, other people?

_____

_____

_____

Are there changes you need to make to increase solitude or being with people?

_____

_____

_____

Never Tried; Never Thought Of

There may be hobbies or recreations you thought might be fun back home, but you never tried them. What were those possibilities you thought of once upon a time?

_____

_____

_____

Is there any chance those hobbies or recreations could work for you here and now? If so, which ones?

_____

_____

_____

What recreations have you seen the local populace or other expatriates engaging in— that you might try?

_____

_____

_____

When I was little, my parents were not stargazers. But in my adolescence we moved to a sub-Sahara country. The heat was sweltering. There was, frankly, not a lot my parents could do for fun, given their location, their six children—and no babysitter. In that country, roofs of houses were cement, and flat. It was remarkably dark at night, with thousands of stars visible. So after the children were in bed, my parents took a blanket up on the roof, lay down, and looked at the stars. They ordered maps of stars that came in the mail, and learned the constellations of the southern hemisphere. They told us kids the names of stars they sighted, and the stories of constellations they found. To this day, they know the stars and constellations of the southern hemisphere better than the northern ones.

Who gave them this idea? I don't know. Maybe the StarMaker.

Hobbies and recreations can cost money, time, and effort—or they might not cost much at all. Whatever they cost, they return to you—in physical and mental well-being, in knowledge of your adopted country and people, in relationships and influence and joy—much more than they cost.

Ask the StarMaker for ideas for recreation in your new land.

Ask Him what good gifts He is waiting to give you.

> *"The Lord be exalted, who delights in the well-being of his servant."*
> *—Psalm 35: 27b NIV*

chapter 5

The Seven Day Workweek Never Was God's Plan

Two seminary professors asked to speak with me privately during a retreat for cross-cultural workers. They looked haggard and embarrassed. After they cleared their throats awkwardly, the story came out: they worked long days and evenings, teaching classes, grading papers, doing administrative duties. In the past year they had been assigned even more classes, more students, more responsibilities, and vacations had been canceled. In addition, they both served churches on weekends. They had wives and families who needed them, too.

The symptoms they reported were classic for depression and burnout: they were deathly tired, but couldn't sleep; they felt lethargic, but agitated. They couldn't concentrate and were forgetful. One of them had heart palpitations, the other a nervous tic in his cheek. They no longer felt interest in their work—or anything they used to enjoy. They felt hopeless and despondent. Now they were being asked by their leadership to do even more.

I sent them to their medical doctors for thorough checkups, and told them that not only could they not "do more," but if they didn't take at least a semester of sabbatical for complete rest, they could damage their health irreparably.

THAT IS A TRUE STORY. I wish it were the only story I have about overwork and burnout among God's sojourners, but it isn't. After receiving nineteen calls to help cross-cultural workers deal with the results of overwork, I stopped counting.

But these people were neither stupid nor irresponsible—the two seminary professors and other international workers who arrived at burnout were simply responding to multiple pressures from their external and internal environments.

See if any of the pressures they responded to, listed below, sound familiar to you. Put a check next to the pressures that could result in times of overwork for you.

☐ The task is urgent: people need to hear the Good News before it is too late. Many of them also need humanitarian aid urgently. It is hard not to respond to need.

☐ The task is never-ending: there are always more people to help.

☐ The work schedule is unpredictable and undefined.

☐ Other colleagues are working as hard, or harder: taking time off causes guilt.

☐ International workers believe if they take time off, critical tasks won't get done.

☐ International workers have a strong work ethic: working hard is seen as honorable.

☐ A clear sense of accomplishment can be hard to come by.

☐ The cost and logistics of arranging time off are daunting.

The road to burnout is paved with the best of intentions.

In each of the 19-plus situations in which I was called in as a professional to help international workers recover from burnout, the workers had to withdraw from ministry for three, six or twelve months in order to preserve their health. In some cases, health was recovered; in others, full return to health was not possible: cumulative overwork and stress had done irreparable damage.

Be careful to preserve your physical health. It is a trick of the devil, which he employs to deceive good souls, to incite them to do more than they are able in order that they may no longer be able to do anything.
—Vincent de Paul (1581-1660)

It is those experiences that cause me to challenge sojourners to build workable patterns of Sabbath and rest into their lives.

If you build such patterns into your life early in your sojourn and diligently maintain them, you will likely never have to withdraw from ministry due to burnout.

Rest Was God's Idea

You don't have to expend a lot of effort, however, in coming up with a plan for getting rest and avoiding overwork. God himself has provided us with a workable plan, designed with our well-being in mind. He gave us the best possible way to counteract the pressures that cause us not to rest: *obedience to His Word and following His example.*

After God was done creating the cosmos and the beautiful world we live in, He rested "from all his work. And God blessed the seventh day and made it holy, because on it he rested from all the work of creating that he had done" (Genesis 2:2, *The Message*).

It is hard to imagine that the Almighty would need rest, but He rested. He made that seventh day of the week special: set apart, as a principle and example. From the very beginning He built into the fabric of the universe a rhythm of work and rest that He wanted us to pay attention to.

When God got His own people, Israel, out of slavery in Egypt and began to shape them into a nation that reflected His values and character, He gave them the Ten Commandments. The fourth commandment says: "Remember the Sabbath day by keeping it holy. Six days you shall labor and do all your work, but the seventh day is a Sabbath to the Lord your God. On it you shall not do any work" (Exodus 20:8-10, NIV).

The fourth commandment conveys an expectation that God's people owed Him the Sabbath, i.e., they were freed from the distractions and burdens of work in order to focus on Him. In Exodus 16:29 there is also the implication that God gave His people the sacred obligation of Sabbath as a gift that was good for *them*. It was a day of blessing: for rest and play and worship.

Sabbath also served as a sign of God's covenant with His people: it set them apart from other nations—who had no weekly day off for rest and worship. In addition, Sabbath was designed to be a weekly reminder for God's people: a reminder of what He had done for them and to whom they belonged.

Sabbath was what God demanded as obligation—and also generously gave. Isn't that typical of God—that what He demands is for our good?

I don't know committed Christians who think it is okay to violate the other nine commandments—to lie, murder, steal, covet, commit adultery, worship idols, or take God's name in vain. But I know many who ignore the Sabbath.

Why is that?

_____

_____

_____

What do you believe about the Sabbath?

_____

_____

_____

I'm aware that some people think of Sabbath as an Old Testament concept, not to be taken seriously today. Jesus himself, however, did not suggest that idea. He appears to have observed the Sabbath himself (Luke 4:16), although He eschewed the stringent legalisms the religious leaders of His day had attached to Sabbath (Matthew 12:1-13).

"Do not think that I have come to abolish the Law or the Prophets;" Jesus said, "I have not come to abolish them but to fulfill them" (Matthew 5:17, NIV). In fact, Jesus' attitude toward the Old Testament laws about adultery, murder, lying, vengeance, prayer, and fasting (Matthew 5:27–6:18) was that mere legalistic observance of the letter of the law in each case was not good enough. Instead, Jesus said that what His Father wants goes way beyond mere observable compliance to those laws. God, Jesus explained, wants a pure heart, strongly devoted to the _full intent of the law_—not only the outward behavior.

> _"The Son of Man is Lord of the Sabbath," Jesus said, referring to himself (Matthew 12:8, NIV)._

Given how Jesus treated other laws and commandments, how do you think He would want you to treat Sabbath?

_____

_____

_____

Have you practiced Sabbath in the past? If so, how?

_____

_____

_____

If you are not sure whether Sabbath is important as a principle for you to include in your life, I invite you to give the matter serious thought. You are welcome to use the Bible references listed at the end of the chapter, and resources listed in the Bibliography.

Living Out the Sabbath

After studying God's Word, as well as commentaries and Christian writers, I have decided that Sabbath keeping is something God expects me to pay attention to and honor, but not legalistically. Everywhere I have lived, regardless of the culture or work schedule, I've learned to set aside a day for worship, rest, and play, a day in which work issues—as much as possible—were not allowed to intrude.

I try for my Sabbath to be a twenty-four-hour period, since that is the model God gave, but sometimes that isn't possible. Depending on work and obligations, the Sabbath day may be a Sunday, but sometimes it is a Saturday, or half of a Monday and half of a Thursday.

At times the day I hope will be Sabbath gets set aside due to a crisis, or a demand I feel God would have me respond to. But I still try to get my Sabbath later.

I don't think there can be a formula for carving out Sabbath in ministry that will work all the time even for one individual, much less for everyone. No formula I know of could be consistently applied for months at a time, nor be flexible enough for the unique demands of serving others in a foreign culture. So flexibility—not legalism—is in order. But it is flexibility prayerfully exercised on the basis of a strong commitment to obey God's principles: an obedience and obligation that blesses and heals me.

I always come away from Sabbath grateful. I may have begun it tired and grumpy, wondering how I'm ever going to catch up on work, especially if I take time off. But Sabbath corrects my perspective: I am reminded that the work I have been given is not my work; it is God's. The success of any work is not my success—but His. Sabbath reminds me of God's goodness and reminds me to trust Him—and that trusting Him is the most important work I do.

Sabbath serves not only as valuable rest and much needed worship, but as an essential reset of paradigms that somehow get out of whack in the course of the week.

The suggestions that follow in this chapter are based on my own experience in learning how to honor Sabbath in the midst of a demanding and constantly changing lifestyle. They are also based on having worked with scores of God's servants trying to do the same. The suggestions are not prescriptive. Only you can prayerfully decide how you are going to honor Sabbath in your life. But the suggestions will help you know what others have tried, and what has helped.

What Happened to Those Sabbath Plans?

In our home cultures, many live by an agenda or schedule of some sort, with meetings, appointments, and commitments planned ahead of time. But often other personal priorities, such as spending time with God, spending time with a spouse or friend, and getting rest aren't written down or planned for a specific time. They are left to fend for themselves, fitting in where convenient.

We assume we will make time for those truly important things, but as life and schedule fill up, we find the supposedly high priorities pushed out into the edges of our lives, and then disappearing altogether.

The solution is to prayerfully think through our schedule and plan for the highest priority items first—choosing an actual day and time when they will happen. Let the lesser priorities fall into the cracks or get pushed off the schedule page.

What are the activities that are of highest priority to you? List at least five, and try to list them in order of priority. Please also put the number of hours per week you want to spend in those activities:

_____

_____

_____

Now take a piece of paper or create a file and begin to think and plan. Since you probably have work or study obligations you are already committed to that are not negotiable, put those down on your schedule. Given that those hours are taken, how will you now fit in Sabbath? Or devotional life? If you are married, when will you have quality time with your spouse?

Whatever else is of high importance, carve out appropriate time slots for it on your weekly schedule, *and write it down.* Those time slots are now taken! Let the rest of life fall in where it can. If someone requests that you do something in a time slot that is taken, you may legitimately reply that you have a commitment. You do.

As much as possible, view the time slots for your highest priorities as sacred. Those time slots can be moved around, or changed, but only for very good reasons.

If you are married, or have a close partnership with a colleague, both partners should agree to the priorities and scheduling. And both partners should have to agree to significant changes.

Creative Ways to Sabbath

God gave His people, Israel, the seventh day of the week as Sabbath—our Saturday. There is evidence that the early church treated the first day of the week (our Sunday) as a day for worship and rest. For many people, Sunday is an ideal day for rest and worship: they can attend church, worship, and spend the rest of the day in ongoing worship and recreation. If Sundays work for you in this way—wonderful! Just try to make sure work-like worries and activities don't creep in to undo the purposes and benefits of Sabbath.

For many busy pastors, doctors, nurses, and others who must work on a Sunday, there is clearly a need to find another day to serve as Sabbath. If Sunday is a workday for you, and you can move your Sabbath to another day of the week, by all means, do so. If Sunday is only partially worshipful, or partially restful, try to find another half day of the week that you can set apart for worship and renewal.

In some countries and cultures the populace (or part of it) observes a day that is different from other workdays for religious, political, or pragmatic reasons. If that day, although not a Sunday, can work as Sabbath for you as a cross-cultural worker, go ahead and use it.

Carving Sabbath out of a weekday if your partner, spouse, or school-age children have week-day commitments may require extra creativity. If Sunday and Saturday are not workable as Sabbath, and children need to be homeschooled or transported to and from school on other days, then parents need to negotiate a schedule whereby the children's needs are met, but each parent is freed up to have at least a few hours of time for soul and body refreshment.

> *A married couple involved in refugee work approached me in severe burnout. For a number of reasons, it was not possible for them to withdraw completely from the country or from ministry. Their Sundays were full of obligations that could not be delegated. Also, it was critical not to disrupt the lives and schooling of their five children. Yet both husband and wife badly needed rest.*
>
> *After much discussion we devised a plan whereby three or four of the couple's duties were delegated or canceled, but not all of them, and not the Sunday ones. We agreed that the wife would shoulder all household and ministry duties during the day on Monday, allowing her husband day-time hours for rest and study. The husband did the same for the wife on Tuesday. Another morning of the week the husband and wife had Sabbath time together. One evening a week the family set aside as family night for fun and worship.*
>
> *It took months—and much negotiating—to get this plan to work, but finally it did. Last I heard, this family was doing well. Needless to say, their Sabbath plan keeps changing—but they have one!*

Sabbath = ?

God's main requirement for Sabbath expressed in Genesis 2:2 and Exodus 20:8 was that His people *should not work* because the day was set apart for Him. In fact *shabat*, the root of our word Sabbath, means *to stop, to desist, to cease from doing*, i.e., abstain from whatever your *work* is.

Whatever your work is, whatever you are tired of—don't do it on the Sabbath. Whatever wears you out and distracts you from God is what you need to abstain from. (That includes language study and computer work if those tasks have made you tired.)

Instead, do what refreshes and renews you. Do what helps you refocus on God and enjoy Him. Many of the rewarding activities you thought about in Chapter 4, including exercise and excursions, can be things that you do on your Sabbath.

Research studies confirm that it helps to vary what we do. If the bulk of your work involves using your mind in study, thinking, writing, then it will be restful for you to do something artistic, something out in nature, or activities that use your body.

If your work involves intensively being with people, then optimally, rest for you will involve solitude—or at least being away from the kind of people who characterize your work.

Conversely, if much of your work is done in solitude, being with people may be refreshing.

If your Sabbath tends to be a Sunday, and your life has been overflowing with people, it is possible that the best way for you to rest and worship is to do so away from other people. You may rest and worship better by yourself, or with just your spouse or a good friend. I think that is okay to do occasionally.

But Leviticus 23:3 shows God adding another dimension to Sabbath: "There are six days you may work," He said to Moses, "but the seventh is a Sabbath day of rest, *a day of sacred assembly.*" Assembling with others who help us remember and praise God's goodness is important—either as part of our Sabbath or part of our week.

Granted, in some situations, where believers are far from other people of like faith, it may not be possible to assemble (except via technology), or perhaps there are only a few other believers to assemble with, and not very often.

 But generally and where possible, we should gather in sacred assembly with others of like faith for mutual encouragement and worship.

What do you need to do and not do on your Sabbath right now in your life?

_____

_____

If you have children at home, how can you as a couple ensure that each of you gets the rest and worship you need, while not neglecting your children?

_____

_____

Before Sabbath Begins

Sabbath will not happen without commitment and planning: not only does it need to be scheduled and that time defended, it needs to be prepared for in the days that precede it.

Remember when God gave the people of Israel manna? He told them to gather it every day, but on the day before the Sabbath they were to gather twice as much manna because it would not be given on the Sabbath (Exodus 16:21-25). They had to plan ahead—and so do we.

Plan in advance for your Sabbath: delegate duties; figure out how to avoid phone calls and messages that disrupt. If your normal tasks include meal planning, cooking, and cleanup, think about how to make those chores as simple and easy—or absent—as possible. Protect your Sabbath by advising others that you will be unavailable, or by making yourself invisible or inaccessible.

What are ways you can prepare ahead of time so that your Sabbath is truly restful and not interrupted?

_____

_____

_____

What if One Day of Rest Is Not Enough?

There may be times in your sojourning life when even the regular observance of Sabbath is not enough rest. This happens because cross-cultural life is innately stressful and the intense demands use up our reserves, leaving us with an energy deficit.

> *Ruth diligently observed Sabbath—she worshipped, rested, and abstained from work. But the strains of managing construction projects she had underway, the intense heat of her adopted country, the stress of constant obstacles and delays, the bleak landscape, and limited recreational options eventually took a toll on her energy.*
>
> *"Take three days off—completely off," I urged her. "Just rest: garden, read, sleep. If after three days of complete rest, you don't feel better, I want you to make an appointment with your doctor for a complete physical. If a physical and lab tests don't show a cause of your fatigue, then I'll recommend more rest time and meeting with a pastor or counselor who can help you explore why your body and soul are not thriving."*

If you are tired: rest. Don't keep pushing yourself. Try two or three days of complete rest, as I suggested to Ruth, and see if that helps. Three days of rest can do wonders and cost much less than other remedies that may have to be tried later if resting is not tried first.

If you find that even with faithful practice of Sabbath, you feel ongoing fatigue, how would you go about clearing your schedule to get three days of rest?

_____

_____

God Gave Extended Time Off

Did you know God gave the original extended time off?

When the people of Israel were in the desert and God was teaching them how to be *His* nation, He not only gave them the Ten Commandments and other laws and regulations, He also gave them holy days—holidays—and weeks of feasting and commemoration.

God told Moses, "Speak to the Israelites and say to them: 'These are my appointed feasts, the appointed feasts of the Lord, which you are to proclaim as sacred assemblies'" (Leviticus 23:1-2). The feasts God gave to His people were:

Passover	1 day
Unleavened Bread	7 days
First Fruits	1 day
Weeks	1 day
Trumpets	1 day
Atonement	1 day
Tabernacles	7 days
Sacred Assembly	1 day
Purim	1 day

If you add up the days God designed for His people to be commemorating, celebrating, feasting, and worshipping, the total is twenty-one days. Some of the feast days, it is true, occasionally overlapped a Sabbath day. Also, a number of the feasts and holy days involved preparation and travel time. In all then, God's people were instructed to take more than twenty-one days off from normal work.

Many Christian people do not celebrate those ancient Israelite holy days today, and I'm not advocating that anyone do so. *What I do want to point out* is that it was God's design for His people to take extended time off from work to commemorate, celebrate, worship, and rest.

When is your next period of extended time off? _____

If you haven't yet begun to plan, what would be restful for you? Would you like to stay home? Go somewhere? If so, where?

_____

_____

_____

How much money can you spend? _____

If you have no money saved for time off, what can you do now that will set money aside for a time of rest?

_____

_____

_____

Obstacles to Observing Sabbath

As mentioned in the introduction, there are a number of pressures on international cross-cultural workers that make it hard for them to carve out time for the rest they legitimately need. Some of those pressures come from the external cross-cultural environment. Others are internal—in the head or heart of the sojourner.

Let's concentrate for a moment on the external obstacles to Sabbath and rest: they come at the sojourner in the form of expectations, requests, or demands from others; or they may be cultural traditions in the adopted country that impact the sojourner's ability to schedule rest.

What expectations, requests, or demands from others might impact your ability to plan effective Sabbaths and other kinds of rest?

_____

_____

_____

What can you do about such expectations, requests, or demands?

_____

_____

_____

Are there cultural traditions in your adopted country that make planning Sabbath and times of rest particularly challenging? If so, what are they, and how can you _appropriately_ work with them, around them, or in spite of them to get enough rest?

_____

_____

_____

In order to avoid burnout, you may need to prayerfully learn how to say a courteous, firm, and culturally appropriate "No."

Internal obstacles to engaging in the rest you need are the ones in your own mind: guilt you may feel when not working, unreasonably high standards you have for your own performance, or comparing yourself to others.

Getting rid of such internal obstacles requires soul searching and prayer.

If you feel guilt when taking time for rest, you'll need to ask yourself, and God, if the guilt you feel is appropriate per His standards, or comes from violating ideals internalized from other people (e.g., parents or teachers).

Guilt comes when we feel our behavior is incorrect. But the standard may be what is incorrect. We need to ask ourselves, "Which is it?"

If the standard is correct, then guilt is appropriate and we need to change our behavior. If the standard is not correct, we need to throw out the standard—and the guilt.

I was once given a bookmark that said, "Excellence in everything." After a while, I threw it away because I decided that excellence in everything was not a reasonable goal to live by. Instead I learned to thoughtfully evaluate the standards I held myself to: only a few activities and duties deserve the time and effort required to achieve the highest standard of excellence. Other tasks, I believe, need to be done reasonably well, but not perfectly.

> *If the standard is correct, then guilt is appropriate and we need to change our behavior. If the standard is not correct, we need to throw out the standard—and the guilt.*

Obviously, such decisions are a matter for individual prayer and reflection. The decisions that result from prayerful thinking should then reflect the Lord's personalized guidance in stewardship of time and energy.

What standards might you be holding yourself to that are not wise or reasonable?

_____

_____

_____

_____

_____

Are you comparing yourself to others—their energy level, their need for rest, their level of accomplishment—in ways that are not appropriate or helpful? _____ If so, what do you feel the Lord would say to you?

_____

_____

_____

_____

Rest Requires Trust

It takes trust to rest: trust that whatever work we are leaving unfinished will be okay in God's hands. We also must trust that we will be accepted and loved even if our work is imperfect or incomplete—*or if we ourselves are imperfect and incomplete.*

You see, while we are still working away, we can persist in the illusion that if we keep striving, maybe we will get it right, maybe the work will be good enough. Maybe, if we do the work well, we ourselves will somehow get to be good enough.

Pausing to rest forces us to recognize that neither our work, nor we ourselves, are going to be good enough—ever. But we are still loved. Even in our incompleteness, with work not finished, we are loved. More than that, we are given the gift of rest—because God is good, and because the work is His to take care of.

The idea of working constantly in order to be successful—or in order to be loved—did not come from God. It may have come from our culture, or our family, maybe, but not from Him.

Instead, here is what God role-modeled for us: He did a stunning bit of work, creating our universe; then He stopped, evaluated what He created and pronounced it good; then He rested.

That's the model He gave us: work hard, stop, evaluate, rest.

He didn't say, "Rest only if the work is done." He just said: "Rest on the seventh day." He appeared to mean, "Whether the work is complete or not, stop and rest—for Me, and for yourself, too. Do it as a sign that it is My work and you can rest in Me."

Make sure you're following God's guidelines for how hard to work and how hard to rest—not anyone else's.

Don't put more pressure on yourself than God does.

Jesus said, "Come to me, all of you who are weary and carry heavy burdens, and I will give you rest. Take my yoke upon you. Let me teach you, because I am humble and gentle at heart, and you will find rest for your souls. For my yoke is easy to bear, and the burden I give you is light."
—Matthew 11: 28-29, NLT

Bible References for Further Study

Genesis 2:2	Isaiah 58:13-14
Exodus 16:21-23, 27-30	Matthew 5:17–6:16
Exodus 20:1-17	Matthew 11:28–12:14
Exodus 31:12-17; 34:21; 35:2-3	Mark 2:23–3:6
Leviticus 23	Luke 6:1-11; 13:10-17; 14:1-6
Numbers 15:32-35	John 5:1-18

Bibliography

Barton, Ruth Haley. *Sacred Rhythms: Arranging Our Lives for Spiritual Transformation.*Intervarsity Press. 2006.

Buchanan, Mark. *The Rest of God: Restoring Your Soul by Restoring Sabbath.* Thomas Nelson. 2006.

Dawn, Marva J. *Keeping the Sabbath Wholly: Ceasing, Resting, Embracing, Feasting.* William B. Eerdmans Publishing Company, Grand Rapids, Michigan. 1989.

Ortberg, John. *Soul Keeping: Caring for the Most Important Part of You.* Zondervan. 2014.

"Sabbath." *The New Bible Dictionary.* Wm. B. Eerdmans Publishing Co., Grand Rapids, Michigan. 1974.

Muller, Wayne. *Sabbath: Restoring the Sacred Rhythm of Rest.* Bantam Books. 1999.

chapter 6

Retraining the Brain: in Small Patterns and Large Paradigms

"Love the Lord your God with all your passion and prayer and intelligence" (Matthew 22:37, The Message).

As a sojourner you are intelligent enough to cross cultures well: it just may not feel like it in the early months. Instead, you may feel your intelligence has taken a severe beating. But be encouraged: it is typical for a new sojourner to feel awkward, stupid, and clumsy.

Your intelligence level is the same as always; your brain is just overburdened by how much there is to learn. Also, part of what you learned in your home culture or in other cultures may not help, and often hinders. Any sojourner's brain, therefore, requires retraining.

The first kind of brain retraining an international worker needs occurs in the first weeks and months in the new country and involves the cognitive principle of *automaticity*—which will be explained shortly. The sojourner needs to be patient with his or her brain until automaticity can make life easier.

Understanding the principles of automaticity can greatly help the sojourner who is attempting to learn a new language. Paying attention to one's learning style can be helpful as well. Finally, monitoring the amount of time a sojourner spends in his or her native language and in the new one—and in switching back and forth—can also help save wear and tear on the brain.

Once the sojourner has mastered a number of basic brain patterns related to daily living, he or she can pay more attention to the mysteries of social interaction. The perceptive sojourner will notice that assumptions about people and behavior that worked back home don't work now. The sojourner needs to deal with the attendant discomfort and learn new paradigms.

This chapter provides an overview of the above themes, with tips and suggestions for how to make the most of the brain's ability to retrain itself—while crossing cultures.

Automaticity

I remember early in my Costa Rica sojourn feeling like my brain worked in slow motion. When I needed to pay for something, I would peer at the coins in my hand, mystified: it took long minutes to figure out what each coin was worth and how to pay for something. Sometimes honest shopkeepers took mercy on me, gave me back what I had given them, and helped me give them the correct amount.

Waiting for a bus, I had to remember the name of the route I needed, look carefully for that name, fight the crowd to get on, pay the correct amount of fare, and remember the stop I needed and the procedure for signaling that I wanted to get off.

When shopping for groceries, I had to decipher the names of items, translating in my head. It was often not clear if the name on a bag or can was a brand name, or the actual ingredient. In some shops, I needed to ask for what I needed, which meant knowing the word in Spanish, and saying the amount I wanted in kilos or liters. This required mental math plus new vocabulary. Needless to say, grocery shopping took an inordinate amount of time and energy.

The Lord God created the human brain with a marvelous ability: automaticity. Automaticity refers to the brain's ability to process something automatically, without having to think about it. Once one repeats a pattern of thought or action enough times, the procedure becomes automatic. Once the brain sequence is automatic, the person may not even be aware that he or she is doing the automatic procedure, and will be able to devote his or her attention to something else.

Did you ever set out to do an errand and without thinking about where you were going, end up at work or school instead? That's automaticity at work!

Typical patterns of behavior that many of us do automatically include: reading, typing, driving, walking, climbing stairs, riding a bike, getting dressed, and operating machines and tools we are familiar with.

In fact, the brain's ability to carry out an operation learned so well that it is now automatic is so efficient that if we try to interfere with the automatic sequence, we slow it down. This happens, for example, if a person has learned how to drive a stick shift vehicle, and then thinks about what gear to use and how far to put in the clutch: thinking about the process can cause a grinding of the gears.

The same thing happens when we are happily typing away. If we pause to think about which keys our fingers are on, or how to spell something, we will slow down our typing.

Such a marvelous ability God gave us! We just don't realize how many sequences of our behavior are on automatic. We barely think about them as we go about everyday life—until we move. *Then we feel slow, unusually stupid, and exhausted* by the incredible number of tiny decisions we have to make—just to figure out how to pay for something or how to get home.

Much of the exhaustion of the first few months of living in a new culture is due to the fact that normal processes of life—getting dressed, getting out the door, finding out how to get somewhere, managing the currency, or figuring out basic vocabulary are not yet *automatic*.

The sojourner's poor brain has so many detailed decisions to make in any given hour that the brain—and hence the sojourner—becomes fatigued.

This is normal!

What are everyday sequences of behavior that are *new for you*—and not on automatic yet?

_____

_____

_____

Are there behaviors or activities in your new country that are beginning to become more automatic for you? If so, what are they?

_____

_____

_____

Be encouraged! The more you engage in the behaviors that seem arduous and time-consuming because they are not on automatic, the sooner they will become automatic. And life will become a bit easier.

Speeding Up the Process

You can help certain sequences of behavior become automatic more quickly by intentionally practicing them in less pressured situations.

Remember when you learned to drive? A responsible adult no doubt took you to an abandoned parking lot or quiet neighborhood, and told you each move to make: "Put your seat belt on, start the car, put your foot on the brake, now put the car in gear, now put your foot on the gas … no, not that hard …" And so on. You did those behaviors, in the correct sequence, over and over again until they became automatic. Then you tried them on a quiet street, then on a busier one. Or else, you took a driving class. But the learning process was the same: small, basic steps repeated in a private, non-threatening environment until they were well rehearsed.

Apply those same principles of practice to whatever you need to learn in your new environment:

☐ Study your currency, and practice using the coins and bills until you know them well. Practice making change until it becomes comfortable.

☐ If you need to use the metric system, memorize the conversions: feet to centimeters; miles to kilometers; gallons to liters; and Fahrenheit to Centigrade, until the conversions happen automatically when you need them.

☐ Look up in a dictionary, or learn from a bilingual friend, the vocabulary you need for grocery shopping or getting the car serviced. Make a note on your phone, on an index card, or in a small notebook you keep handy. In time you will use your prop less and less.

☐ When learning a new language, there is simply no substitute for memorization: memorize verb conjugations, rules of grammar, and vocabulary. While memorization requires energy and time, it produces automaticity much more efficiently than random learning, and ultimately reduces fatigue and frustration.

☐ If you need to learn how to navigate a route by car, bus, or foot, practice doing so when you aren't in a hurry, and it doesn't matter if you make a mistake. When you have traversed the route correctly once, practice it one more time to fully engrave the sequence in your brain.

The brain is so amazing that you can even practice things in your head, without physically doing them. Imagine driving a route, or making change with currency, or engaging in other behavioral sequences *in your imagination.*

Can this help? Yes! Sports psychologists have athletes do this to prepare for competition. The psychologist will recommend to a cross-country skier, for example, that she learn the race route by actually skiing the terrain. Later, the skier will be instructed to follow that route in her imagination, visualizing the curves, remembering the feelings in her muscles, watching out for certain hills, and mentally practicing how to respond to hazards or conditions. The mental practice helps the athlete respond more automatically in the actual race, freeing up her attention for other eventualities.

God gave you a brain that can put well-rehearsed sequences of behavior on automatic. It is a wonderful ability. Make the most of it by helping your brain repeat and practice what needs to be learned.

This should give you great hope because soon you won't have to struggle to think about what coins or bills to use, or what vocabulary you need, or how to get somewhere. You will just do those things without even thinking about them—just as you used to do many things back home.

What thought or behavior patterns do you hope will soon be automatic?

_____

_____

_____

What might you do to hasten the process of those patterns becoming automatic?

_____

_____

_____

It will be nice to have more of your brain back! You will need it for other learning.

Language Learning—and Automaticity

Learning a new language is a subset of the principle of automaticity, for in learning a new language you must acquire hundreds, maybe thousands, of new neuronal patterns, until they are so automatic that you speak that language fluently.

As a baby and toddler, you learned your own native language randomly, gradually picking up the patterns of verb conjugations and semantic sentence structure over time. You weren't in a hurry, and people were patient with you. In fact, they probably acted like you were a genius when you put new words together. And—you were!

Unfortunately, no one will treat you like a genius now that you are an adult learning a second or third language. Although it does take a great deal of intelligence and effort.

The good news is that you do not have to learn this new language randomly, as toddlers do. Most likely someone is teaching you the logical and predictable patterns of nouns, verbs, pronouns, and semantics—not to mention pronunciation.

The second piece of good news is that if you *practice* the different components of the new language, those components *will* eventually become automatic. Repetition is what makes the forms of language become automatic for you. Some people have to practice more than others to get things on automatic. But the principle of automaticity works—eventually—for everyone.

Language Learning and Your Learning Style

Besides practicing, practicing, and practicing, you can help yourself learn a new language by paying attention to your own learning style preferences.

Some authors have suggested that there are three basic learning styles: visual, auditory, and kinesthetic. Others suggest four styles, or seven, and still others various combinations of styles.[1]

It is not important to review learning style theory here, nor spell out the different kinds of learning styles authors say there are. It seems like common sense to recognize that some people learn best:

- when material is presented visually.
- through their ears, e.g., from lecture, being read to, or having material set to music.
- through stories and illustrations.
- when presented with facts and logic.
- from reading on their own and organizing facts by taking notes and outlining.
- when their bodies are actively involved and moving: being hands-on, or through dance, drama, or sculpture.
- in a group: the lively interaction helps them think and remember, while trying to learn alone seems boring.
- in private, quietly memorizing, practicing, or drawing, until they have the concepts figured out, and can bear trying them out in public.

Most of us probably do not learn in any *one* style, but have several styles that we prefer—or at least that we have adapted to.

What are your own most preferred styles of learning? What learning methods have worked best for you in the past?

_____

_____

_____

Based on past experience, what are your least preferred or less effective ways to try to learn?

_____

_____

_____

How does what you have just self-reported about your learning style affect how you learn a language?

_____

_____

_____

You may have little choice regarding the kind of teaching style available to you as you learn your foreign language: there may be a limited number of language schools in your area, or that you can afford. Possibly, in your situation, the best way for you to learn the language is with a tutor.

I am not advocating that you try to change the instructional style of the person or institution that is helping you learn the foreign language. That would probably not be helpful. I *am* advocating that you—yourself—be aware of what works best for the aspects of learning *you* are responsible for. For example, if you have homework to do and it helps you to hear it out loud, then use a recording device and listen to yourself, or have someone record sentences, vocabulary, or stories for you. If it helps you to write things over and over, or outline, or draw, or act them out, or create games and puzzles that motivate you—do that.

If you learn best in the company of others, do what you can to form a study group. If you learn best by yourself, try to find privacy and quiet.

There is no ideal or perfect learning style. We are just made differently, and we need to cooperate with the way we are made. But we need to stretch ourselves, too.

So be willing to embrace the opposite of your preferred style as well.

> _Ben and Michael both started in language school at the same time. Mornings they had structured classes in phonetics, grammar, vocabulary, and conversation. Afternoons were free for them to study._
>
> _Ben used his afternoons to be out and about talking to people. He seldom sat and studied. As a result, he learned many words, slang, sayings, and jokes, but his use of verb tenses was abysmal and his sentence structure shaky._

Michael used his afternoons to study on his own. He memorized verb conjugations, grammatical structure, and vocabulary assiduously. As a result he learned the language well, but was hesitant to talk in public.

Ultimately, teachers praised both Ben and Michael for hard work and excellent progress, but they told Ben he would not pass the final exam unless he hired a tutor to help him with verb tenses and grammatical construction. Ben did so. Michael's teachers praised his knowledge but forced him to preach in public, lead small groups, and pushed him out into the streets to practice.

Today, more than a decade later, host country colleagues would rank both Ben and Michael's linguistic performance as roughly the same quality—but with profoundly different styles. Not surprisingly, their personal styles still characterize their linguistic performance. Michael lectures, preaches, and writes beautifully, in a somewhat formal manner. He does well in daily conversation, too. Ben is less formal, but is known for his wit and humor, knowledge of local slang, and storytelling.

Both Ben and Michael are respected and loved. They arrived at a deep love of their new language and culture by very different routes, but they worked hard—and got there.

Know your preferred learning styles and apply them to the aspects of language study over which you have control. But be willing to embrace the styles that are less comfortable for you as well.

Be a Steward of Your Brain

Attention span

The human attention span is only about fifty to fifty-five minutes long, I learned in a Cognitive Psychology class I took a number of years ago. Current research, according to Wikipedia, suggests that older children and adults have a sustained attention span of about twenty minutes.[2] Other authors suggest different attention span lengths.

Whether your attention span is fifty minutes or twenty, know your own capacity, and when your attention wanders, by all means try refocusing. Experts call this attention renewal.

But after you have renewed attention several times, take a break. Just a short break away from your current task (two minutes, five minutes), giving attention to something completely different, helps your brain. Your concentration will be better and you will be more productive when you go back to the previous task.

In the process of writing this book, for example, I take breaks every hour or so. I get up, look out a window at the view, pet my cat, put a few dishes away, water a plant, do some stretches. Then I get back to work with renewed energy and focus.

Be a good steward of your brain's resources: take short breaks as you need to, but don't get distracted for long. When your brain feels really fried, take a longer break of half an hour or an hour. You will work more effectively if you do so.

How long do you think your normal attention span is? _____

Is there a time of day, or a location, in which your attention spans seems to last longer?

_____

What are some activities you can use to refresh your brain without getting unduly distracted?

_____

_____

_____

Compartmentalizing

In Chapter 2, on stress management, I encouraged you to lower stress by *not* switching from one language to another throughout your day—at least in terms of written or technological tasks.

If you live in a foreign country and are learning a foreign language, you *will be* constantly thinking in one language or the other, switching back and forth or translating in your mind. That is inevitable—and not a bad thing. But it will reduce the drain on your brain if you limit your engagement in your native language on your phone, tablet, or computer to specific time periods during the day or week. You could, for example, confine your reading and responding to social media, e-mail, and Skype in your native language to Tuesday, Thursday, and Saturday evenings between seven and nine.

Loving the Lord with all your mind means making the best possible use of your intelligence—and also knowing when to let your brain rest.

Have mercy on your brain! Let it function and build relationships in one language at a time as much as you reasonably can. While you need to stay connected to your home culture to a degree, the more brain space you allocate to your new language and culture, the more quickly you will become effective and at home there.

Loving the Lord with all your mind means making the best possible use of your intelligence—and also knowing when to let your brain rest.

Retraining in Major Cultural Paradigms

Ashley stood in a long line inside the bank, carefully not crowding the person in front of her. But the umbrella of the person behind her kept poking into her back. She could smell the faint odor of the man, he was so close.

"Why is he standing so close to me?" she wondered. "Does he think that by crowding me he can make the line move faster? I hate having him so close to me! I feel intimidated, invaded. What should I do? Should I leave and come back later? But I hate to waste all the time I've spent in line already!"

Ashley doesn't know this yet, but leaving the bank line and returning later will not help. She is a sojourner in a country where it is ordinary for people to have a small personal space bubble. What she is experiencing in the bank line has nothing to do with the man behind her being in a hurry, or pushy, or intimidating—and everything to do with the invisible space bubble he is accustomed to—and Ashley is not.

In every culture, people grow up learning—unconsciously—how close to get to people who are not in their circle of intimates. Certain family members, spouses, children, or pets may be exceptions to that space bubble rule: they can get close to the individual with impunity. But people outside that special circle should only approach the outer edges of the invisible space bubble.

The problem is that, depending on the country, that space bubble may have a diameter of 12 inches, or 18, or 24. Usually, we are not even aware of our home culture's bubble size until we suddenly feel someone has stepped inside it. Then we think they are pushy, intimidating, or trying to be too familiar. Conversely, if someone stands too far away by our unconscious standards, we may feel they are standoffish, aloof, trying to avoid us, or perhaps, trying to get away.

The invisible space bubble that all cultures have is an excellent example of cultural paradigms we learn as we grow up, yet are often unaware that we are internalizing. We only become aware of our own assumptions about proxemics (the use of space) if we engage with a foreign culture, feel the discomfort that attends the operation of a different paradigm, and work hard to understand what the cause of our discomfort is.

International workers often make the mistake of ignoring or avoiding that sense of discomfort instead of trying to understand what is different. They can easily make an erroneous assumption about what has happened—as Ashley did when she thought the man behind her was pushy when actually, it was Ashley's own assumptions about personal space that were causing her discomfort.

The space bubble is only one example of many cultural paradigms that we hold unconsciously, but that profoundly affect how we react when people in our host country don't behave the way we expect them to.

A few of the other cultural paradigms we might encounter are: how the culture handles time, how honesty and truth are managed, how male and female relationships are navigated, or how authority and power are leveraged. The list is long. It is normal to be ignorant—in the beginning.

How Can One Learn the Paradigms of a Foreign Culture?

There are easy ways and the harder way. Usually an international worker learns as much as possible by the easy ways, but ends up learning, inevitably, the hard way as well.

Easier ways:

1. Read as much about your host country's culture as you can. If there are books written about the cultural assumptions and mores—read those. Read the history of the country; and the literature of the country: the poems, the novels, the ballads. Listen to the music of the country.

2. Find a cultural guide you trust and ask them to explain what you don't understand. Finding a good cultural guide is admittedly tricky. An expatriate who has been in the country for years, who speaks the language well, who has a deep love and respect for the culture, and is loved by its people can be an excellent guide. A person from within the culture, however, may not be able to explain cultural assumptions to you, any more than the man in the bank could have explained to Ashley why she felt he was standing too close to her; from his perspective, he was behaving normally. A person from your host culture might be of help to you, however, if he or she is well educated and has lived in a culture not their own long enough to develop insight into cross-cultural paradigms.

The hard way:

In his excellent book *The Art of Crossing Cultures*,[3] Craig Storti does a beautiful job of explaining the typical way—and the harder way—most sojourners learn the cultural paradigms of their adopted country. I will summarize Storti's most salient points:

1. We expect others to be like us, but they aren't. In other words, we expect them to share, and operate by, our own cultural assumptions, but they often don't.

2. When they don't, a cultural incident occurs. A cultural incident can be any interaction that reveals to us that a cultural paradigm different from our own is in operation. For Ashley, it was the incident in the bank line.

3. The cultural incident causes *a reaction in the sojourner*. The reaction could be anger, fear, annoyance, or surprise. For Ashley it was mild annoyance and a sense of panic.

4. The sojourner's natural reaction to a cultural incident is *to withdraw*. Unfortunately, many sojourners withdraw, and that is all they do. They withdraw from as many cultural incidents as they can until they ultimately stop interacting.

5. Ideally, however, the sojourner becomes aware of his or her withdrawal, and of the emotional reaction that has caused that withdrawal.

6. The sojourner then reflects on the *cause* of that emotional reaction.

7. The emotional reaction then subsides.

8. The decrease of emotion allows the sojourner to reflect on the cultural incident, trying to understand what happened.

9. As the sojourner begins to understand the cultural paradigms operating in the host country that have caused the discomfort, he or she begins to develop culturally appropriate expectations.

Let's use an example to apply Storti's principles:

> *My husband wanted to host a dinner for about twenty-five people. I willingly agreed to prepare the meal, planning to serve it buffet style, since we could not possibly seat twenty-five people at a table. The day came, the blessing was said, the food was laid out on the buffet, and I invited everyone to come and help themselves. But nothing happened. I invited them again. There was an awkward pause. Finally, the women in the group got up and served the men, then served themselves.*

Cultural incident! In that quiet pause I realized I had done something culturally inappropriate by serving buffet style. My emotional reaction was embarrassment and puzzlement.

But as I thought about the whole experience, I realized that our guests had appreciated being invited to our house; I think they forgave me my *faux pas*. As my embarrassment subsided, I thought about how meals are typically served in that culture: the mother, grandmother, or cook is the only person who knows how much food there is available and how many are being fed. Thus the cook, knowing how to ration the food, serves the plates accordingly. The head of household and any male guests, siblings, or sons are served first, and given more.

Once I figured all that out, I understood how I had confused my guests, and I knew what to do. The next time I served a meal to a crowd of people in that country, I served the plates and had a helper pass the plates out. I developed culturally appropriate expectations and behaviors!

You will experience many cultural incidents. At least—I hope you do! And you may feel puzzled, hurt, irritated, angry, or intimidated. The feelings are natural: don't be critical of yourself for having the feelings.

Recognize and accept the feelings and then move past them to wonder what happened.

Ponder the situation, try to figure it out, ask a trusted person if appropriate. In time, you will begin to understand the underpinnings of the culture, and learn how to operate in it appropriately. That's the beauty of it.

Please describe cultural incidents you have experienced so far:

_____

_____

_____

What have you learned from such cultural incidents?

_____

_____

_____

If you need help understanding what happened, who might serve as a good cultural guide?

_____

_____

_____

Your brain can be retrained—even in those large cultural paradigms that are unconsciously learned in childhood. As you cross into another culture, learning which of your cultural assumptions fit with the new culture and which ones don't can cause discomfort.

Embrace the discomfort: it is the cue that learning is needed; it is an important part of beginning to retrain your brain.

An invaluable book for helping international workers understand the cultural paradigms that buttress different cultures is *Foreign to Familiar*, by Sarah Lanier.[4] I highly recommend it. While the process of learning about cultural paradigms as a sojourner will almost always involve those uncomfortable cultural incidents, Sarah's book can save you a great deal of pain.

But Should We Always Adapt?

There are almost certainly cultural values or paradigms in your own home culture that you do not agree with or conform to.

My home culture, my passport country, is the United States. While there are many cultural paradigms and values of my country that I enjoy and am proud of, there are others I don't agree with. A typical value of U.S. culture is that more is better: a bigger house is assumed to be better, making more money is better, supersizing your fast food meal is better, and so on. Certainly, not everyone in the U.S. agrees with that value, but I think it is fair to say that the paradigm underlies much consumer behavior. Well, I don't agree with that value, and try not to live by it. It doesn't fit with how I interpret the commands of Jesus.

It should not be surprising then, that you or I might also disagree with cultural values we discover in an adopted country. For example, the bigamy or bribery that are ingrained parts of a number of cultures may be values that international workers will not be able to adopt or become accustomed to.

So as you feel the discomfort of a cultural incident, and begin to reflect on the cultural assumptions that are the foundation of what you perceive, you may have no trouble adapting to the values and behavior patterns of the culture. At other times, you may find that rather than adapting to your adopted culture's way of doing things, you will choose *not* to adapt.

It is absolutely critical to take time to think through such issues carefully. If you are a follower of Christ, I believe you are responsible to prayerfully, carefully think about which cultural values to adapt to—and which ones not to buy into: *in your adopted country's culture—and in your own home culture as well.*

In fact, sometimes coming to understand a cultural paradigm of your adopted country might make you rethink a paradigm of your home culture—and make you wonder whether how you have been thinking and behaving is in line with what God wants. That's the value of brain retraining.

Are there cultural paradigms you have discovered in your adopted country that you feel you cannot adapt to? If so, which ones, and why?

_____

_____

_____

Are there cultural paradigms or values in your home country that you have chosen not to follow? What are they?

_____

_____

_____

Are there cultural paradigms you have discovered in your adopted country that have made you rethink values and assumptions of your home country? If so, which ones?

_____

_____

_____

The Holy Retrained Brain

Your brain is imminently retrainable. It is the Lord who made it that way and who wants to accompany you as you learn new thinking, behavior, and values.

You can learn new sequences of thought and behavior—repeating them enough so that they become automatic. Then you'll do those new tasks quickly and unconsciously.

You can master a new language, taking advantage of that ability to memorize verb conjugations and vocabulary until they become so automatic that you speak whole sentences without thinking about the verbs or the nouns.

It would be wise to give your brain a break—by pausing for rest when your attention span is exhausted. Help your brain out by understanding your own learning style and making the most of the methods that work for you. Reduce brain drain by switching between languages only as much as necessary.

Increase your awareness of the mysterious paradigms of your adopted culture by reading as much as you can about it, finding a cultural guide, and by embracing those uncomfortable cultural incidents that can be the springboard to valuable learning and adaptation.

Above all, invite the Holy Spirit to be your guide as you learn the values that guide human interactions in your adopted culture, so that you learn quickly and adapt well—or choose not to adapt—in ways that honor the One who called you.

> *"Be transformed by the renewing of your mind. Then you will be able to test and approve what God's will is—his good, pleasing and perfect will" (Romans 12:2 NIV).*

Footnotes:

1. *https://www.thoughtco.com/three-different-learning-styles3212040; https://learning-styles-online.com; http://www.edudemic.com/styles-of-learning/; http://www.learningrx.com/types-of-learning-styles-faq.htm; http://en.wikipedia.org/wiki/Learning_styles*

2. *http://en.wikipedia.org/wiki/Attention span*

3. Storti, Craig. *The Art of Crossing Cultures.* Intercultural Press. 2007

4. Lanier, Sarah. *Foreign to Familiar: A Guide to Understanding Hot-and Cold-Climate Cultures.* McDougal Publishing, P. O. Box 3595, Hagerstown, MD. 217423595. 2000.

chapter 7

Who Am I Anyway? Rediscovering Identity in a New World

A CURIOUS THING OFTEN HAPPENS in the first year of sojourning: our identity seems to morph, shift, or disappear. This can be merely disconcerting, or downright shattering.

Brent and Kara have been in their new country for a number of months. Kara is doing well at the language, but their two-year-old and four-year-old have been repeatedly sick, whiny, and irritable—which makes her feel like a failure as a mother. In addition, she has learned that her nursing degree will not be accepted by the local Nursing Association. This means she cannot practice, teach, or lead in her profession as she had hoped. She feels incompetent as a parent, and useless in her profession—the two areas of identity most important to her.

Brent, meanwhile, has struggled more than Kara in language learning. That alone has been hard for him. A position as professor is urgently awaiting him as soon as he is linguistically competent, but preparing even one hour of lecture takes him six hours and the help of a translator. At present he cannot imagine taking on even a half-time teaching load.

Both Brent and Kara are deeply discouraged. They wonder if God can use them in their new environment at all.

While some identity confusion is a normal part of cross-cultural adjustment, it often comes as a surprise. Perhaps no one warns us about it because, although many international workers have experienced the phenomenon, it is not easy to put into words. Or perhaps we don't hear much about it because people who have been overseas for a few years evolve a new identity and forget how confusing it was in early days.

If you sojourn for any significant period of time, you will find your old identity no longer quite fits or makes sense. But if you stay in your adopted country, and work at it, the search for your new identity can bring about significant growth:

1. It can result in a deeper understanding of who you are on a number of levels.

2. It can result in a deeper understanding of how the culture you came from formed your identity.

3. It can help you understand identity constructs in the new culture.

4. It can result in a deeper understanding of your spiritual identity.

Before we delve into why reconfiguring identity can be uncomfortable, let's figure out who you used to be.

Who Were You?

There are three major conceptual ways to think about one's identity: in terms of relationships, in terms of roles and achievements, and in terms of status. All three are important, and of course, the concepts interact with each other. How important each element is in conceptualizing identity differs greatly from culture to culture.

For right now, please think about your identity as it was in your most recent home culture.

1. Let's tackle relationships first

Please list the relationships that have been important in defining who you are—for yourself, and also for how others perceive you. Include family, professional, community, or spiritual relationships:

_____

_____

_____

2. Now for roles and achievements

Please list the roles you performed in the last few years before you moved overseas. Think of job titles you had, things people expected you to do, and achievements you were proud of:

_____

_____

_____

Think over your list for a moment: Which roles were most fulfilling? Which achievements or roles gave you the most prestige? Which roles have been left behind? Which roles came with you to your new country? Which roles do you miss?

_____

_____

_____

Which roles were, or are, most important to your sense of identity, of who you are?

_____

_____

_____

3. Status is the position or rank of a person in relation to others.

What status would you say others perceived you as having in your home culture? One way to express status would be in terms of lower class, middle class, or upper class. Where do you think others would have placed you on that continuum?

_____

_____

_____

Where would you have placed yourself?

_____

_____

_____

How about in terms of education? Would others have viewed you as uneducated, highly educated, or somewhere in between?

_____

_____

_____

In your previous life in your home country, although you had the relationships, roles, and status you have noted above, you probably did not think much about your identity in those terms. You were who you were, did the best you could do, and most of the time felt fairly competent.

As you adjust to a new culture, however, relationships and roles may have changed and status may be perceived differently. The process of adjusting to these changes can undermine anyone's sense of competence.

Sense of Competence

Adjusting to a foreign country is challenging, and few of us do it as well as we hoped, or as well as we would like to. In the adjustment process our sense of competence usually takes a hit.

We find ourselves stressed; we miss things from home. We don't know our way around, and have to learn arduously by trial and error. We grieve our losses—slowly. We miss important relational cues, causing awkward cultural incidents. Even sojourners who are gifted at language learning make many mistakes. It seems to take *forever* to become functional—much less fluent or effective.

In our new location we become aware, over and over, that people around us do not know who we are, and for the most part, don't care. The whole experience of not being known and feeling incompetent is quite, quite humbling. Not feeling valued is deeply discouraging.

And then there are our attitudes: how irritated we get with foreign people we don't understand, or who don't understand us; how frustrated we become with government or service systems that don't work as we think they should; or how annoyed we become with those we live with.

We get discouraged with how little progress we make. Or we feel pride that we are doing better than someone else who is trying just as hard, and then feel ashamed of our pride. What happened to the competent person we left behind? What happened to the spiritually mature person we hoped we would be?

What happens to us in the process of cross-cultural adjustment is like what happens to a piece of antique furniture when it is stripped.

Stripping a piece of furniture involves applying a strong chemical that eats away layers of old stain and varnish; then the residue is scraped off. The wood is sanded over and over; sometimes a chisel is applied to particularly deep stains. Only when smooth natural wood is all that can be seen is the piece of furniture ready for new stain and varnish—its new identity.

It is the same piece of furniture, but ready for a new life.

The process of stripping applied to a human being, however, is painful.

Brent and Kara, in our opening story, were experiencing just such stripping of their identities and sense of competence. If, right at that point, someone had handed Brent and Kara one-way airline tickets back to their home country, they would have been strongly tempted to get on the plane.

Most sojourners have at least one day—some have many more than one day—in which they are so humbled by the stripping process of cross-cultural adjustment that they feel utterly useless.

What happens to us in the process of cross-cultural adjustment is like what happens to a piece of antique furniture when it is stripped.

They wonder if they can make it, or if they should just quit. They wonder if God can use them—at all.

Wondering if God can use us is actually a good thing. Not only do most godly sojourners get to that point—it is essential, spiritually.

When our old identity, based on known roles, relationships, and achievements is stripped away, we get down to the bottom of ourselves. We get to nobodyhood. When we get to nobodyhood, we are forced to stop relying on our own sense of worth, or what others think of us. Hopefully, we then turn, instead, to Christ, and find our worth and identity in Him.

I wish we could turn to the Lord for our sense of value just once and have the issue forever settled, but usually it is a process: over and over again when we feel incompetent, like a nobody, we need to stop looking at our roles, or the opinions of others for our sense of value, and turn to God instead.

> *"Live in me. Make your home in me just as I do in you. In the same way that a branch can't bear grapes by itself but only by being joined to the vine, you can't bear fruit unless you are joined with me" (John 15:4, The Message).*

Most sojourners who have journeyed overseas out of service to God did so because they believed they could "help God's cause." But sometimes, after a period of stripping, they not only question whether they are much help, but wonder if, in fact, they might be a hindrance.

"Does God need me?" they wonder. "Would His cause be better off without me?"

Should they then buy a ticket home?

Not before asking two important questions:

One is, "Does God, in fact, need any of us to accomplish His work?"

Scripture tells us clearly that *God does not need us* to do the work He wants done. He can accomplish anything He wants without us. But in His marvelous grace, by His chosen design, He has given us the privilege of serving Him. We are His workmanship, "created in Christ Jesus to do good works, which God prepared in advance for us to do" (Ephesians 2:10, NIV). And "our competence comes from God" (2 Corinthians 3:5, NIV).

> *The great thing about the identity stripping process of sojourning is that it keeps us on our knees—where we need to be anyway.*

Therefore, whether we feel competent or not, whether we feel God needs us or not, we need to obey Him. We need to be engaged in the good works that He has created us to do, trusting Him for the strength and ability to do what He wants.

Concentrating on obedience shifts the focus from our own sense of incompetence to how God sees us and who He wants us to be. It shifts the focus from our inadequacy to His provision. It is our need to obey Him and trust Him that is most important. If He has called us to be in a particular place, doing a particular task, then whether we feel competent, needed, recognized, or valued is not relevant. We need to obey.

If obedience is the key, then the second question we should ask before boarding an outbound plane is: regardless of how we see ourselves, *what does God want us to do?*

God could steer us away from working internationally by helping us learn we cannot do something well, or by helping us realize that a particular assignment could end up harming us or someone else. But it is equally possible that He wants us to embrace nobodyhood, trusting Him to provide what we need to accomplish the goals He has for us. It is critical to make such an important decision based on trust and obedience—not on our own sense of competence.

The great thing about the identity stripping process of sojourning is that it keeps us on our knees—where we need to be anyway.

Have you sometimes questioned your effectiveness as a sojourner? What situations, experiences, or issues have caused your questioning?

_____

_____

_____

If you have felt less competent than you used to; if your previous relationships, roles, and status are affected by living in a foreign country; if you are no longer sure what your identity is, may you find comfort, value, and guidance in seeking the Lord and trusting Him.

But let's also try to understand what—besides feeling less competent—is making you feel that way, and what elements of identity will factor into who you will become.

Foundational Elements of Identity

Zack, living in a foreign country, thinks of himself as having sacrificed a lot to be there, and expects to soon make a valuable contribution in his new location by opening a bookstore where people can not only buy interesting books, but discuss important questions of faith and culture. He spends most of his weekends planning for and praying about the future project with friends who think like he does.

His host country neighbors think of Zack as rich, because although he lives modestly in their neighborhood, he has an expensive phone, camera, and computer. They think he is a person of leisure because all he seems to do is study their language. When he is gone on weekends, they assume he is having fun. They know of his plans for a bookstore, but hold a wait and see attitude, wondering why he wouldn't establish a bookstore in his own country, and sometimes ask each other if perhaps Zack works as an undercover agent for his government.

Back where Zack came from, his friends think he is some kind of super- spiritual, altruistic hero who was crazy to have thrown away a potentially prestigious career.

Is Zack who his foreign neighbors think he is? Is Zack who his friends back home think he is? Or is Zack who *Zack* thinks he is?

Three foundational elements of identity that are important to understand are:

1. the interaction between who we think we are and who other people think we are.

2. the fact that, in forming concepts of identity, some cultures focus more on relationships and other cultures focus more on roles and achievements.

3. the *status* of an individual, then, could depend more on relationships in some cultures, and more on roles or achievements in other cultures. In each culture the exact mix of elements that determines status is unique. The perception of status can also depend on the socioeconomic level of the person doing the evaluating.

An international worker adjusting to another culture therefore needs to ask himself or herself, "Am I from a more relational culture? Or from a culture that focuses on roles and achievements?" And, "What kind of culture am I trying to adapt to?"

In a relational culture, an individual's achievements matter—whether educational, athletic, or professional—but not as much as the individual's family history, tribe, or ethnicity.

> *A young African man is seen herding cattle. A foreign observer would be unaware that he is the son of a tribal chief with considerable land holdings and political clout. The young man sees his identity more in terms of his family than his job.*
>
> *In a Latin American country, a sojourner could enter a hardware store and meet a woman who seems to be the manager, but spends most of her time talking with people who come into the store but make no purchases. Only later might the sojourner realize this lady is a former mayor, currently unable to run for office because of a quirk in the electoral system. Her family owns the hardware store as well as 30 percent of local real estate. She may not appear to be working much, but those who come in to chat with her are making the deals that will decide the future of the city.*

In a culture that focuses more on roles and achievements than on relationships, a young woman may be the daughter of a famous lawyer or of a down-and-out drug addict, or she may come from an affluent neighborhood in Boston or a ghetto in New Orleans, but her reputation and status depend more on the fact that she won an Olympic bronze medal or graduated *summa cum laude* from Harvard than on her family or geographical background.

What do you think? Is the culture you grew up in more relationally oriented, or more role and achievement oriented?

_____

_____

_____

What about the culture you are adapting to? Is it more relationally oriented or more role and achievement oriented?

_____

_____

_____

So Who Are You Now?

At the beginning of this chapter you gave some thought to the relationships and roles that used to define who you were back home. And you guessed at others' perceptions of your status there. Most likely, those constructs remain in your head, at least residually, as a definition of who you are. But how do your current roles and relationships factor into your identity now? How do you come across to people in your host country?

1. Roles:

What roles are you currently engaged in, in your land of sojourn? Or what roles do you hope to take on in the near future?

_____

_____

_____

Which of the roles you just wrote down are understandable to your host country neighbors or colleagues without a great deal of explanation?

_____

_____

_____

2. Relationships:

What relationships do you currently have that would be understandable to your host country neighbors or colleagues in terms of understanding your identity? Include family, community, and collegial relationships. Don't forget affiliations with groups or agencies that might be known to those around you:

_____

_____

_____

Of the relationships you wrote down, which would seem most prestigious or important to your identity for residents of your host country?

_____

_____

_____

3. Status

What do you think your perceived status is in your new country? Are you thought of as lower class, middle class, or upper class—as poor, affluent, or in-between?

_____

_____

_____

Are you perceived as uneducated, highly educated, or somewhere in between?

_____

_____

_____

In your opinion, is the perception of your status in your host country different from the perception others had of your status back home?

_____

_____

_____

4. General Perceptions

How do you think your host country neighbors or colleagues would describe you?

_____

_____

_____

5. Your Reaction

How do you feel about the probable perceptions of those around you regarding who you are?

_____

_____

_____

How would you like to be perceived?

_____

_____

_____

Dealing with Misconceptions of Identity

What if we will never be seen as we would like to be seen in our adopted country?

> *When we lived in Colombia, my husband worked with poor people in job creation programs. He was constantly asked for money, even though he repeatedly explained that he could help people create small businesses, but had no funds to give away. I teased him that he must look like a rich guy. For Christmas I gave him a T-shirt that read, "Yes, I'm a foreigner, but no, I don't have money." He never wore the T-shirt in public, but it helped us chuckle at a constant, irritating misunderstanding of who he was and what he was trying to do.*

Have you tried to correct misperceptions of who you are in your land of sojourn? Describe such situations and how you felt about them:

_____

_____

_____

How important is it to correct another person's misconceptions of our identity? *The answer is: it depends on whom we are doing the correcting for.*

If we wish to correct someone's misperceptions of us so that we can feel better about ourselves, and that is the principle reason, then it is not necessary to do the correcting. We need to learn to live with being misunderstood—thought of as *less than* or *other than* we are.

But if the other person's misunderstanding of who we are could be harmful for *them* in any way, if their misunderstanding of us could hurt a future relationship, or result in personal or spiritual harm *for them*, then we should try to correct the misunderstanding. Also, if the misunderstanding could harm the reputation of a person or group we are affiliated with, then it is important to correct the misconception as diplomatically as possible.

However, once Jesus had corrected misperceptions of His identity, He allowed people to make their own choices about who they thought He was.

Jesus is our example in dealing with misperceptions of identity: He was completely comfortable in His own skin—knew exactly who He was. But the crowds who swarmed around Him saw Him as a celebrity who could do miracles and wanted to make Him into a political revolutionary. The religious leadership of His day saw Jesus as a threat, accused Him of blasphemy and wanted to get rid of Him.

For himself, Jesus was unaffected by such misconceptions. But He did correct the mistaken perceptions of His audience because those people needed to know the truth about Him.

However, once Jesus had corrected misperceptions of His identity, He allowed people to make their own choices about who they thought He was.

After spending months with His closest disciples, Jesus one day asked them point blank who they thought He was. Peter correctly identified Jesus as Christ, the Messiah (Mark 8: 29), but a few seconds later got the rest of Jesus' identity all wrong by objecting when Jesus began to explain His role as suffering servant who came to die.

At that point Peter interrupted Jesus, protesting that he didn't like or want the sacrificial identity Jesus was describing, and Jesus had to rebuke Peter strongly (Mark 8: 33).

After rebuking Peter, Jesus went on to explain that not only was His identity one of serving, suffering, and being misunderstood even to the point of death, but that He expects the same identity in His followers:

> *"If anyone would come after me, he must deny himself and take up his cross and follow me. For whoever wants to save his life will lose it, but whoever loses his life for me and for the gospel will save it" (Mark 8:34-35, NIV).*

The Apostle Paul, following in Jesus' footsteps, also had to deal with misunderstandings about who he was. "I care very little if I am judged by you or by any human court," he wrote the Corinthians, "indeed, I do not even judge myself … It is the Lord who judges me" (1 Corinthians 4:3-4, NIV). And:

> *"If anyone else thinks he has reasons to put confidence in the flesh, I have more … But whatever was to my profit I now consider loss for the sake of Christ" (Philippians 3:4, 8, NIV).*

Jesus' example, and Paul's, teach us that we should try to be unaffected by people's misconceptions of who we are, and only correct their misconceptions when doing so will help *them*. Apart from helping others toward truth about us for their own wellbeing, we need to die to our own need to be understood or seen as important, leaving our identities in God's hands.

This is easy to say but very hard to do. I find that whenever I feel like explaining to someone who I really am, or wishing to defend my importance, I have to stop and think about whether I'm doing it for them—or for me. I often need to go back to the scripture passages cited above, and ask the Lord's help in getting over myself, leave my identity and value in His hands, and be content to be misunderstood—or at least, not as understood as I would like.

Needless to say, this is a lesson that is constantly re-learned.

A special word on gender-related expectations:

Both men and women need to be extremely sensitive to gender role expectations as they move into a new sub-culture or culture—whether at home or abroad. But since more cultures tend to be male-dominated than female-dominated, women, even more than men, may experience identity confusion as they try to take on roles in a new environment.

If a woman is accustomed, for example, to acting in a professional capacity or leadership role in her former life, but moves into a situation that does not accept women in such roles, then she may experience resistance, criticism, and confusion. She may become frustrated.

Both female and male international workers need to exercise discretion and gentleness as they take on roles—feeling their way carefully and asking for advice so as not to offend and alienate. This requires humility and patience.

For further understanding of important gender and relational issues in crossing cultures, I refer you to Sarah Lanier's excellent treatment of this subject in her book *Foreign to Familiar*, Chapter 7.[1]

Figuring out how to tactfully take on new roles is challenging. So is figuring out how and when to correct other people's misconceptions of us. Even harder is prayerfully learning to be content with not being understood.

Your best recourse—and mine—every time, is to go *home* in our minds—not to who we used to be, not to some previous identity or hoped-for identity, but home to the One who created and called us.

Who You Really Are

You are and always will be God's dearly loved child, bought at stupendous cost, guided and tenderly cared for every step of the way. He has work for you to do that He will give you the strength and competence to do. That is the basis of your identity.

Slowly, as you trust and patiently wait, you will be led into relationships and roles that will define how you are perceived by others and what you can offer your adopted country. Gradually, a new identity will evolve.

Will those new relationships, roles, and perceptions be *you*?

No. Just part of you. You will still have relationships that remain invisible to people in the country of your sojourn. There will be roles you used to have that remain part of you in some way, even if they are not known in your adopted country.

And someday when you go back home, there will be new pieces of you, roles and relationships, a language, customs, patterns of thought, that are not known or recognized by people at home. Your identity will have even more parts. You will have become even more complex!

Each of us is like a many-faceted jewel. Facets of my identity jewel relate to having grown up in Africa, or having lived in Latin America or the United States. I have identity facets as a wife, others as a mother, still others as a sister, daughter, psychologist, teacher, writer, and friend. No one fully understands all my facets. I feel fortunate when I am with a person who resonates with at least a few of them!

No one will fully understand each of your facets either, much less all of them. Except God. He cut each facet. He has a use for each facet. He enjoys all your facets, wants to shine through all of them. Your combined facets are designed to reflect Him as no other jewel can.

Wrapping Up Identity

As you wrestle with the identity issues that surface in the process of cross-cultural adjustment, be willing to face the hard and messy questions. Allow some of your facets to be hidden and unrecognized. Be willing to be misunderstood, and thought of as less than you are.

Be willing, also, to engage in the hard thinking that is essential for deciding whether to correct a person's misconceptions of you—or not.

Be willing to undergo the painful stripping away of your sense of competence and self-worth—down to the nobodyhood that teaches deep dependence on your Savior.

This process of questioning and understanding identity as a sojourner is going to take a while—so be patient with yourself. In fact, it will probably recur and continue to some extent throughout your life.

So you are almost done with this chapter, but you are at the beginning of a valuable process of reflecting on and evolving a new identity. I hope reading this chapter has helped you understand better what you are experiencing, and that it is a normal part of cross-cultural adaptation. I hope you now have a better handle on how to think it through—and especially, how to pray it through.

It is a good and necessary process because it clarifies what—or who—we are dependent on for our sense of value and purpose. Who we are is best grounded in *whose* we are.

> *I took you from the ends of the earth,*
> *from its farthest corners I called you.*
> *I said, "You are my servant;"*
> *I have chosen you and not rejected you.*
> *So do not fear, for I am with you;*
> *Do not be dismayed, for I am your God.*
> *I will strengthen you and help you;*
> *I will uphold you with my righteous right hand.*
> *—Isaiah 41:9-10, NIV*

Bible References for Additional Study:

Psalm 16	1 Corinthians 9:19-27
Psalm 139	2 Corinthians 12:1-10
Mark 8:31-17	Ephesians 2:8-10
John 15:1-17	Philippians 3
Acts 17:24-28	Hebrews 11

Footnotes

1. Lanier, Sarah. *Foreign to Familiar.* McDougal Publishing, P. O. Box 3595, Hagerstown, MD. 2000.

chapter 8

Eye of the Storm: Connecting with God amid Turmoil

Dan was deeply immersed in his video game, chasing the elusive enemy. He hadn't noticed, but it was well past midnight. His wife, Karen, had gone to bed long ago; the kids were sound asleep. Dan was just about to annihilate his target when a pop-up blocked his view. At first, he was annoyed, but the tag line made him laugh, so he scrolled farther down. Soon he was looking at content he knew he should not see. He stared at the screen a moment, and then tore his eyes away, to the wall above his computer. At first his gaze was unfocused, but gradually he saw the calendar Karen had put there. The month's verse was: "I am with you always!"

Dan took a deep breath and slammed the laptop closed. "What am I thinking?" he whispered. His mind played over past weeks in which he and Karen, stressed and exhausted, had snapped at each other more and more, and then avoided each other. Karen went to bed earlier, taking a book. Dan escaped into gaming.

They both functioned—took care of the kids, got meals, did the basics of language study and ministry. But they were desperately tired, emotionally numb, and disconnected. It had been a long time since they had had a good talk or shown any affection.

And, Dan suddenly realized, it had been a long time since he had read his Bible or prayed, other than for public duties.

"This will never do," he thought.

Melissa had no spouse to spar with or disappoint. She dutifully read her Bible and tried to pray every day. But it didn't feel like it did any good. She experienced nothing and felt like her prayers hit the ceiling.

Melissa went to all the meetings she was supposed to; she completed her assignments—but like an automaton. "Why do I feel nothing when I read God's Word or pray?" she asked her empty room. "What am I here for, if my spiritual life doesn't give me anything? What is the matter with me?"

I CAN SYMPATHIZE WITH DAN AND MELISSA. It is common to physically survive the hurricane winds of cross-cultural adjustment, but get blown off one's spiritual foundations. If you have been anywhere near a hurricane or tornado, you know how overwhelming it is: the sound and fury of wind and rain make you dive for safety and think only of survival.

The early months of international living are not unlike a hurricane, and the sojourner understandably concentrates on just surviving: staying safe, getting food on the table, learning how to get around. It is easy to forget the most necessary thing of all: staying connected to God.

But getting past the storm is not the key; connecting with the One who is peace and strength in the storm is the key.

"After all," we think, "God will still be there … We'll get back to His Word and praying when we can." As happened with Dan, before we know it, we are spiritually adrift.

Or, if we are like Melissa, we maintain a dutiful routine in the midst of mind-numbing exhaustion, but have no real connection with God.

It is easy to let our connection with God fade, thinking that once the worst of the storm is over, we'll do better.

But getting past the storm is not the key; connecting with the One who is peace and strength in the storm is the key.

Because although the stresses and storms of living overseas may wane, they never completely stop. Periods of intensity and exhaustion come and go as part of sojourner life. So sojourners who follow Jesus must learn simple techniques for staying close to God in the middle of large or small storms. During periods of relative calm, they can go back to building deeper spiritual disciplines into their lives.

In the next few pages we'll look at why practicing the spiritual disciplines during times of stress is hard. Then we'll review two practices we must use consistently to stay anchored. And we'll look at simple, easy-to-implement ways of remaining anchored—even when overwhelmed.

Survival Is Not Enough

For the sojourner newly arrived in a foreign country, trying to learn his or her way around, simply being functional seems like quite an achievement. *And it is.* We have already noted the effects of high adrenaline in the system, the many losses sustained, the emptiness from not having rewarding activities, and the brain fatigue that occurs from too much new information.

All of these demands on the sojourner's system affect spirituality as well: it is normal for the sojourner to feel emotionally and spiritually numb. It is natural to opt for mere physical survival and put off connecting with God until later.

These understandable behaviors, though, affect us spiritually the way not eating or drinking affects our body. It is true that we can fast for several days and still function. But it is not true that we function equally well: we get grumpy, light-headed, and weak. Our stamina and mental judgment deteriorate. If we continue to eat nothing or eat poorly, our physical health deteriorates. Becoming dehydrated, we know, has even more devastating effects: systemic failure, erratic thinking, collapse. The same effects occur spiritually when we don't get spiritual food and drink.

Because our bodies register hunger and thirst, we are unlikely to starve or dehydrate ourselves to the point of physical death.

Spiritually, though, we can starve or dehydrate ourselves into stupefied numbness quite easily.

After reading Dan and Melissa's stories, which story do you connect with more?

_____

Why?

_____

_____

_____

Is your personal prayer life, Bible study, or time with the Lord different in your new country? If so, how and why?

_____

_____

_____

It will not be surprising if your answers reveal that you are not doing as well as you would like. Staying connected to God in the midst of an ongoing storm is extremely challenging.

But be encouraged: tiny changes in behavior can move anyone toward vibrant spiritual health. Just as our physical bodies can survive on small, frequent snacks of protein, and constant sips of water can keep us hydrated—we can learn to keep ourselves fed and hydrated spiritually in small, simple ways as well.

Spiritual ADD

Why are we prone to starving or dehydrating ourselves spiritually?

The truth is, we all have a severe spiritual attention deficit disorder. We are constantly distracted from the reality, comfort, and strength of God's presence. We easily forget to immerse our minds in His truth. It takes constant discipline and effort to reconnect with God.

The dangers of not doing so were illustrated in a study of international workers and sexual temptation. Roughly seven percent of those surveyed succumbed to significant moral failure. Of those who experienced moral failure, all but one were in their first five years of overseas ministry. Subjects in the study reported that internal factors "of the heart" were of greater significance in resisting or succumbing to sexual temptation than external factors.[1]

Keeping our hearts close to God needs to be our highest priority. The devil would love for us to be distracted, drift away from God, and become vulnerable to temptation. The Apostle Paul wrote:

> "Be prepared. You're up against far more than you can handle on your own. Take all the help you can get, every weapon God has issued, so that when it's all over ... you'll still be on your feet. ... God's Word is an indispensable weapon. In the same way, prayer is essential in this ongoing warfare" (Ephesians 6:13-18, The Message).

It is no secret that there is a battle going on and we are in the middle of it. There is no need to expend energy trying to figure out which storm winds are part of cross-cultural living and which are attacks from the evil one. We just need to keep our armor on—which is the same thing as staying anchored.

Why Do We Seek Escape—Instead of God?

If you have gone through a period of stress, you have no doubt noticed that when you can finally take a break, what comes naturally is to escape into a book, a movie, a game—or sleep. What does *not* seem to come naturally is to engage in a few minutes of Bible study or prayer.

But why? Why don't we gravitate toward the spiritual disciplines we need?

You might think I'm going to say it is because we are sinners. We are, but I don't think that is the main reason.

Instead I think that when we are tired and stressed, we want to escape the real world we have been grappling with and *not think about it* for a while. We want relief from reality.

But connecting with God and applying His truths to daily life deals with reality—visible and invisible. In that sense this is hard work, not escape. Connecting with God and living out His truth involves intentionality and effort. So it is understandable that when we're tired and stressed, we want to skip prayer and avoid thinking about His Word.

It is understandable, but we know it is not wise. Heading straight for the relief of escape activities without taking at least a little time to refresh ourselves with God's words and presence is like skipping meals and eating only candy. We know how well that goes.

Escape can be a legitimate means of rest and refreshment—in its place. What I recommend, for myself and for you, is, when we finally have time for a break from reality, we should connect with God first: pray briefly, get His Word into our head—then escape. These spiritual refuelings don't have to take long—it's the connection and focus that matter.

Two Spiritual Anchors

There are a number of spiritual disciplines, depending on whom you consult[2] and I believe we should practice all the disciplines, but which ones we practice, and when, depends on our needs, personal styles, and phase of life.

But there are two main disciplines we all *always* need: 1) to be fed on the truths of God's Word and 2) to be in connection with God through prayer. Both are integral to life as a disciple, and require effort, but neither discipline requires as much time and effort—in the middle of a storm—as we sometimes think.

1. Anchored by Truth

Remember Melissa in the introductory story? She was dutifully reading her Bible, but not feeling anything. Most likely she is mentally and emotionally worn out from the transition she has come through. It might be helpful for Melissa to stop trying to read chunks of scripture and just focus on the salient truth of one verse or phrase. She could try any of the simple techniques described in coming paragraphs. Whatever she tries, it is important for her to realize:

> *She doesn't need to "feel anything" as much as she needs to keep basic truths front and center in her mind.*

There are many, many ways to be fed by the truths of God's Word. Individual Bible reading and study are necessary for every Christian's growth. But there are other ways to be fed on God's Word: listening to sermons, participating in group Bible studies, reading books by Christian authors, listening to podcasts, or listening to Christian music are just a few.

In the past, what has worked for you in terms of ingesting the truths of God's Word? Please include means not listed above, if you used them:

_____

_____

_____

What, if anything, is working now?

_____

_____

_____

Ron learned how to study God's Word in depth as a seminary student and used to love delving into a passage with commentary in hand, digging out the meanings of Greek or Hebrew words, considering the context, and pondering how to apply the truths in daily life. But now that he is overseas, Ron finds that he can't concentrate for long; he doesn't have his commentaries unpacked. He wishes for his old devotional life, but knows he is simply not capable of it at this point.

Kristin longs for her Bible study group back home. More than anything else, preparing for that study, listening to other people's insights, and praying together used to help her be aware of God's truths and primed her to behave in the ways God wants.

Now she feels at a loss.

In early months of living overseas—or whenever life gets stormy—we may not have the mental bandwidth to do in-depth Bible study. We may not have the tools, the props, or the companions we would like to have either—but we have God's Spirit with us to help us garner enough discipline to stay on track.

One of the two disciplines—anchors—we most need is to keep God's truths present in our minds. But we don't have to read long passages or absorb large chunks of theology during times of stress. Leave that for later. Even with a short attention span, we can be centered and grounded in God's truth by doing one or two of the simple things listed below.

☐ Read, over and over, one simple verse or phrase of Biblical truth to absorb the meaning.

☐ Read a verse or passage in different Bible translations; if you are learning a new language, study your verse or passage in that language. Different versions and phrasings can bring new insights.

- [ ] Read a psalm: just one, every day. Ponder it. If a psalm is long, read just a section.

- [ ] Read short devotionals: from a book, booklet, or online resource.

- [ ] Post small cards containing verses of scripture in various places around your home; read and ponder them often.

- [ ] Keep a verse on your phone or on a card in your wallet; review it when you're waiting: for a doctor, a plane, a bus, a friend, or if you can't sleep.

- [ ] Listen to songs that have scriptural content: don't just play the music—meditate on it.

- [ ] Read sermons from books; listen to sermons online. Stop reading or listening when you can't concentrate anymore or if you have absorbed one important truth.

- [ ] Read inspirational books by Christian writers you trust, but read only as much as you can absorb. You may find it helpful to re-read a book that spoke to you in the past.

- [ ] Go out in nature; find a beautiful view. Look at creation and remember who made it.

- [ ] Recall passages about creation, or ones that use metaphors from creation for scriptural truths.

- [ ] Take a Bible passage that uses a metaphor and use your imagination to make the metaphor come alive in your own life (e.g., shepherd, refuge, light).

- [ ] Memorize verses and passages of scripture that contain important truths.

I'm not advocating that you do all of the above things: just choose one or two. Change modalities as you need to.

However, I would like to highlight the value of memorization.

If we want to keep God's Word anchoring our souls and transforming our lives, nothing quite matches the power of memorizing scripture.

In my own experience, memorizing God's Word not only keeps it present in my mind—it also allows those truths to filter down into who I am, changing me. Memorizing helps me ponder—meditate—truly grasp and apply in daily life the meaning of the words and metaphors God has given. As I memorize and chew on God's Word, it soaks into me—and comes alive.

When pieces of scripture are memorized, I can access them easily in the middle of the night, in the middle of a conversation, while I'm doing the dishes—without a book or device as prop. Many times I have had phrases of memorized scripture pop into mind to comfort me, confront me, and steer me.

Memorizing may sound like an old-fashioned discipline, but recent research shows that memorizing and meditation increase gray matter and help us deal more effectively with trauma and stress.[3]

In life's stormy weather, memorized scripture becomes especially needed and beneficial: even a tired mind can spend one minute remembering or memorizing a simple sentence.

Of the above simple ways to keep scripture anchoring your soul during stormy weather, what ways might work best for you?

_____

_____

_____

When you find yourself adapting better to life overseas, please go back to more in-depth Bible study. Or find a group to study with. When you can concentrate more, build on the simple techniques you have been using during a time of stress by using them for longer periods of time: read the entire sermon, and outline it. Memorize longer chunks of scripture. Read a psalm for starters, and then study another passage. Dig out your commentaries.

In a settled lifestyle, you wouldn't be content with snacks as a steady diet; you'd want complete meals of protein, vegetables, fruit, and carbs—not to mention an occasional feast. Just so, when life settles a bit, you will want to engage in full and healthy spiritual disciplines of all kinds, with occasional feasts.

But when storms come up again and your resources are stretched thin, it is good to know how to keep yourself spiritually fed with simple, easy-to-eat spiritual food.

Discover New Spiritual Pathways

For all of us, switching gears in regard to how we ingest God's Word and connect with Him can be helpful—especially in times of stress.

In his book *God Is Closer Than You Think*, John Ortberg describes how different we human beings can be in the ways we approach and relate to God.[4] He suggests we respond to God differently because God himself made us to do so: each of us is a unique reflection of Him.

Our own ways of relating to God make sense to us, but may not seem natural to others and vice versa. It is important then, that we understand what Ortberg calls our own preferred "spiritual pathways," and use them, but also understand other approaches and be willing to try something different.

Ortberg defines a spiritual pathway as "the way we most naturally sense God's presence and experience spiritual growth."[5] I will briefly summarize, below, the seven pathways he describes, but please see Ortberg's book, or *Sacred Pathways* by Gary Thomas[6] if you would like to learn more about spiritual pathways.

Spiritual Pathways:

1. Intellectual: people on this pathway draw closer to God via study and learning. They love theology, books, libraries, and bookstores.

2. Relational: people who follow the relational pathway find a deep sense of God's presence when they're involved in significant relationships.

3. Serving: on the serving pathway, people experience God's presence most tangibly when they are helping others.

4. Worship: the worship pathway is characterized by people who feel something deep inside them released when praise and adoration are given voice, and in music.

5. Activist: activists have a high level of energy; they love to be in action, correcting injustice, and helping change the world for the better.

6. Contemplative: the contemplative person loves large blocks of uninterrupted time, using images and metaphors for prayer and study.

7. Creation: creation pathway people connect with God best when out in nature; being outdoors replenishes and energizes them.

Ortberg says that most of us have one or two preferred spiritual pathways and that each pathway has inherent strengths and weaknesses. That is why it is a good idea to use our preferred methods, but also to try other pathways occasionally. Doing so can also help us be less judgmental of others.

Which spiritual pathways are your preferred ways of relating to God?

_____

_____

_____

Which different spiritual pathways might help you during times of stress, or otherwise help you grow spiritually?

_____

_____

_____

Especially in the midst of life's storms, it may help to try different ways of embracing God's truths and accessing His presence.

2. Anchored by Prayer

"Hi, Dr. Jan!" Jordan flopped down on the couch across from the stocky, gray-haired woman. "The others are held up in the nurses' hall—they'll be here in a bit."

"I'm glad to catch you before the others get here, though," Jordan continued impulsively, "because I've wanted to ask you something! Dr. Jan … I want to know how you do it …" He hesitated.

"Do what exactly?"

"Well, you're always so kind, so calm … even in the chaos of the emergency room with people talking in three languages … or when you're talking to patients…or even how you correct staff firmly, but gently … you always seem not to be in a hurry, and to convey compassion. How do you do that? Were you born that way?"

"No." Dr. Jan chuckled. "I certainly didn't come that way. You should have known me twenty years ago! No, Jordan, seriously, I think the secret is … well, I pray all the time."

"Pray all the time! What do you say?"

"Well," Dr. Jan spoke slowly, "often it's just 'help!' Like, 'Lord, help me get this diagnosis,' or 'help me get the right medications,' or 'help me be kind to this angry person,' or 'help me get where I'm going!'"

"Clearly, He doesn't always answer that prayer!" interjected Jordan, and they both chuckled. Dr. Jan was notorious for getting lost. Jordan and others had learned not to ask her for directions.

"No, He doesn't always answer my prayers the way I want," admitted Dr. Jan, "but even when I'm lost or late, I know He's with me—and loves me. Lots of times I'm not talking to Him, really, not saying anything in words. I just reach out to Him for strength, for help— just kind of rest in His presence." She smiled. "Lots of times I'm just saying, 'Thank you! Thank you for this laughter … this sunrise … this coffee. Thank you for that help. Thank you for loving me."

"How do you learn to do this?" Jordan asked.

"Just start. Turn to Him in your mind. Talk with Him about simply everything. Offer Him every little thing you do. Enjoy His presence; lean on Him. Be thankful for tiny blessings. And don't get discouraged when you forget. Just keep trying."

Other staff began arriving then, so Jordan said softly, "Thanks, Dr. Jan! You know, we all want to be like you when we grow up!"

Any connection we make with God is prayer. Any reaching out to God is a response to the fact that He has already reached out to us: by creating us, sending His son, always being with us.

Like Dr. Jan said, our prayer might be a simple, "Help!" It might be a request, a complaint, a diatribe, a simple "thank you," or a hymn of adoration. Whatever the prayer is, it reaches out to connect with God, and accesses Him. That is what we need, more than anything else—connection with God. The more we connect, the better it is for us.

How are you doing at connecting with God in this time of your life?

_____

_____

_____

Is your current prayer life different from how your prayer life used to be? If so, how?

_____

_____

_____

What would you like your prayer life to look like?

_____

_____

_____

It is true that creating times of solitude for praising God is an excellent spiritual discipline. And extended praying for people who need God's healing, help, or blessing is also part of a healthy prayer life. If you are finding solitude and doing that kind of prayer—good for you. Or if you hope to get back to, or grow toward, that kind of prayer life—wonderful.

But when we're stressed and fatigued, we may not have the mental or emotional stamina for that kind of prayer life. In such times—and frankly at all times—we need to practice some of the behaviors Dr. Jan mentioned:

- Talk to God about whatever is on your mind, whatever you are doing, wherever you are, as often as you can remember.

- Sing to Him.

- Be still before God; quiet yourself, concentrating on Him.

- Use any metaphor provided in scripture and talk to God using that metaphor, e.g., thank Him for being your shepherd, ask Him to be your refuge, ask Him to be your shield, thank Him for feeding you from His living bread.

- Ask Him to flow through you as you do things.

- Ask His help and depend on Him, even when you think you know what you are doing.

- Think of yourself as *in His presence*, resting in that reality, as often as you can.

- Simply *connect with God*. Words are not necessarily needed; simply reach out for His presence. Many Biblical metaphors apply to this reality: holding God's hand, running to Him for refuge, God being our rock, drinking from the fountain of life, abiding in Him (the vine), waiting on Him, walking in His way, hoping in His lovingkindness.

- Ask His help with the current chore: whether that is cooking, studying, or listening. Offer the current chore to Him in worship—after all,

Whether you eat or drink or whatever you do, do it all for the glory of God (1 Corinthians 10:31, NIV).

Of the above ways of connecting to God, which ones already work for you?

_____

_____

_____

Which ones would you like to try to do more?

_____

_____

_____

Are there ways of connecting with God not mentioned above that are meaningful for you?

_____

_____

_____

When your current storm settles down a bit, when you have more concentration and energy, I hope you create larger spaces in your life for solitude and times of intercession, worship, and contemplation—which are like long drinks of cool, life-giving water.

In the meantime, carry around with you the water bottle of on-the-go-prayer and take frequent sips of God-connection in the ways that work for you. Stay hydrated!

Spiritual Maturity = Dependency

Unlike human parents, God does not expect us to grow up and become independent of Him. Self-reliance is what gets us in trouble. Paradoxically, becoming more mature as Jesus followers means becoming more dependent on Him.

It means connecting with God more and more until we are "practicing His presence continually"[7] and "praying without ceasing" (1 Thessalonians 5:17). It means keeping His Word central in our minds, guiding all thoughts and behavior.

So let us grow up—into increasing dependence on God. He is always there, waiting for us to connect with Him, ready to help us live by His truth.[8]

In any hurricane or tornado, the winds swirl around and around a central area of absolute calm. In that "eye" of the storm, the sun can shine brightly on a scene of extraordinary stillness. Because an earthly, geographical storm keeps moving, humans caught in the path of the storm experience the eye as a strange and temporary lull.

Spiritually, however, our God can always provide for us the paradoxical calm of the eye of the storm. Since He is always present with us, His peace and strength are not a temporary lull, but a constant resource.

While we always wish for the storm to calm down, we need—spiritually—to find the eye of the storm more than we need the storm to be over. We need to live in the eye of God's presence and truth always—whatever the wind speed.

It is depending on God that helps us respond appropriately in every aspect of cross-cultural living. In all previous chapters, prayer has been recommended as the key for learning how to resolve or manage the challenges of cross-cultural life:

- _Pray to know when to take a break from stress and when to embrace it as calling._

- *Pray for grace and comfort as losses are grieved.*
- *Ask the Star-maker which recreations to use, and when and how.*
- *Pray about how to build Sabbath and rest and play into a life of service.*
- *Ask for guidance regarding when to adapt one's brain to local customs—or not.*
- *Pray for help in giving up an aspect of identity, or explaining it.*

We just need to pray all the time, without stopping.

The wonderful thing is that God does not resent our dependency on Him: He *delights* in it! Not because He needs anything from us, but because He knows that what we most need is Him. He made us that way.

"The Lord's delight is in those who fear him, those who put their hope in his unfailing love" (Psalm 147:11, New Living Translation).

So make God's day: depend on Him! Keep His Word anchoring your soul; connect with Him as often as you can.

This is a stormy planet we live on, and sojourning is a stormy way of life. The eye of the storm is where we need to stay.

Footnotes

1. "Breach of Great Commission Trust," Project submitted for Doctor of Ministry Program, Bethel Seminary, by Rev. Dennis Ahern, Th.M., October 2009.

2. Richard Foster, in *Celebration of Discipline: The Path to Spiritual Growth*, Harper & Row, 1978, lists 12 disciplines. Dallas Willard, in *The Spirit of the Disciplines*, HarperCollins, 1988, lists 15 disciplines.

3. *www.sciencedaily.com/2009/05/090512134655.htm; http://www.awaken. com/2012/07/in-praise-of-memorization-10-proven-brain-benefits/*

4. John Ortberg, *God Is Closer Than You Think*. Zondervan. 2005. Chapter 7.

5. Ibid., p. 111

6. *Sacred Pathways*, by Gary Thomas. Zondervan. 1996

7. *Practicing His Presence,* Brother Lawrence, Frank Laubach. Library of Spiritual Classics, ed. Gene Edwards, 1973.

8. For more on the topic of practicing the presence of God and living all of life as worship, see *The Sacred Mundane*, by Connie Befus. The book is available on Kindle from Amazon, or in hard copy from the author. Contact cbefus@yahoo.com.

Bibliography

Befus, Connie. *The Sacred Mundane*. 2009. Available from the author at: cbefus@yahoo.com or on Amazon Kindle.

Edwards, Gene. *Practicing His Presence,* Brother Lawrence, Frank Laubach. Library of Spiritual Classics. 1973.

Foster, Richard. *Celebration of Discipline: The Path to Spiritual Growth*. Harper & Row, 1978.

Foster, Richard. *Prayer: Finding the Heart's True Home*. HarperCollins. 1992.

Miller, Robert S. *Spiritual Survival Handbook for Cross-Cultural Workers*. Pioneers, BottomLine Media. 2011.

Ortberg, John. *God is Closer Thank You Think*. Zondervan. 2005.

Peterson, Eugene. *Answering God: The Psalms as Tools for Prayer*. HarperCollins. 1989.

Thomas, Gary. *Sacred Pathways*. Zondervan. 1996.

Yancey, Philip. *Prayer: Does It Make Any Difference?* Zondervan. 2006.

Willard, Dallas. *Hearing God: Developing a Conversational Relationship with God*. Intervarsity Press. 1999.

Willard, Dallas. *The Spirit of the Disciplines*. HarperCollins, 1988.

chapter 9

Beyond Surviving: What It Takes to Thrive

Thrive means to grow or develop successfully; to flourish or succeed; to progress toward a goal—despite or because of circumstances. (Merriam-Webster Dictionary).

THRIVING DOES NOT DEPEND ON EVERYTHING going smoothly; it depends on the ability of the individual to grow and work toward his or her goals even in the midst of difficulty. Thriving, in other words, depends on the response of the person involved—to whatever comes.

Thriving as a sojourner depends on a healthy, balanced use of the spiritual disciplines, stress management techniques and other self-care aids that have been described in this workbook. They are skills any sojourner needs—particularly in their first year of living overseas—but truthfully, throughout any sojourn—and even after that.

This is why it is important to remember that taking care of one's self and working hard for the Kingdom are not competing values: both are an integral part of serving well.

Thriving implies that a person is working hard at the tasks they are committed to, but also taking care of their body, mind and soul. Trying to balance work, ministry and self-care is admittedly tricky: things get out of balance easily and need constant readjustment. The balancing act will always be a work in progress.

This is why it is important to remember that taking care of one's self and working hard for the Kingdom are not competing values: both are an integral part of serving well.

Taking care of one's jar of clay is part of the assignment.

How are you doing at thriving, given the definition above?

_____

_____

_____

A Friendly Test

Below you will find a brief summary of the skills covered in each chapter of this workbook—and then questions that will help you know how well you have absorbed and applied the workbook material. You can use the questions as a kind of "final test" to see how well you are doing.

It is a "friendly test," though, since there will be no grade and no criticism of how you are doing. If you realize you need to improve your skills in any area—that realization will simply be encouragement to keep on praying and growing.

Managing Stress

Stress crops up in any life—but especially while living cross-culturally. When we are stressed we get sick more easily, can't sleep, can't think and in general don't do well. That is why chapter 2 tackled the importance of learning to manage stress. Pacing ourselves, slowing ourselves down, allowing ourselves small breaks for relaxation and joy, getting a little bit of exercise, relaxing our muscles, breathing deeply—these are skills we need whenever we feel stressed—or see potential stress on the horizon.

What scenarios seem to typically raise your stress level?

_____

_____

_____

What stress management techniques have worked best for you?

_____

_____

_____

Loss and Grieving

We miss things when we transfer to a new place, and have to learn to grieve what we miss, as discussed in chapter 3, or we won't have emotional space for new relationships and joys.

What hard work of grieving have you had to do in the recent past?

_____

_____

_____

Recreation

Recreation—hobbies, exercise, play—are necessary for a healthy life and therefore should not be sacrificed as one builds a new life in a foreign country: that was the basic message of chapter 4. Recreational activities can also lay the groundwork for relationships and avenues of ministry.

What recreations have you found to do in your new country?

_____

_____

_____

Sabbath and Rest

The unique challenges of trying to create space for Sabbath amidst the demands of ministry were discussed in Chapter 5. Those challenges were then held up against the need to be obedient to God's design of Sabbath for his people, and his invitation to take time for rest by trusting him for the work he calls us to.

What ways have you found to incorporate Sabbath and rest into your current life? ____

_____

_____

_____

Retraining the Brain

Whenever we change locations or roles our brain has to re-learn the behavioral sequences that were so efficiently put on "automatic" in our previous life. And when we change cultures, our brain also has to become sensitive to the mostly unconscious assumptions about social interaction that drive the host culture. How to adjust to these needs for retraining the brain was the topic of discussion in chapter 6.

In what ways have you intentionally embraced retraining your brain?

_____

_____

_____

Evolving Identity

Figuring out who we are as we move to a new country, give up past roles and experience different degrees of being misunderstood was discussed in chapter 7. The challenges of knowing when and how to correct people's misperceptions and how to be content when we are misunderstood and feel like "nobody" were described. The main conclusion of chapter 7 was that learning how to base our identity in Christ is critical for our long term health and effectiveness as international workers.

What aspects of wrestling with identity or being misunderstood have you experienced and thought through?

_____

_____

_____

Spiritual Life

In the last chapter—chapter 8—about staying connected with God in the midst of storms, I encouraged sojourners to use brief and simple ways of maintaining habits of prayer and keeping God's Word in mind.

What is working to help you maintain a vibrant spiritual life?

_____

_____

_____

Congratulations!

If you have thought of, or written down, answers to the above questions, then: Congratulations! You are taking steps toward—not only surviving—but thriving in your new environment. If you noticed areas in which you still have thinking and learning to do, or behaviors to incorporate—then you know what to do.

As you continue...

In the midst of trying to balance work, ministry and the demands of daily life, this question will constantly surface: should you take care of your own body, mind and soul—or sacrifice yourself for the needs of another or for ministry?

Those are hard decisions to make. I wish there were a nice formula for how to always answer that question, but there isn't. Except this one:

> _Trust in the Lord with all your heart and don't lean on your own understanding; in all your ways acknowledge Him, and He will direct your paths. (Proverbs 3:5-6, NIV)_

As you seek the Lord's guidance, He will show you how to balance working hard with taking care of the jar of clay that holds the treasure of the gospel: the clay jar that is you.

As you depend on Him, He will help you thrive.

Appendix

Case Studies from Real Life:

Showing Workbook Principles Applied Over the Long Term

To SEE WHAT THRIVING LOOKS LIKE over the long haul using the principles presented in previous chapters, take a peek into the lives of international workers Tim and Dana Turner and Kelley Caldwell . (Note: Tim, Dana and Kelley are fictional people, but combine true stories from real life.)

Who They Are

Tim and Dana Turner are international workers sent by their agency at the invitation of an agricultural training center and association of cooperatives in a foreign country. The idea was that Tim would teach a few courses in the training center, help the co-ops with administration and also use his presence and networks to help disciple new Christians there. Tim's past experience in farming cooperatives and in pastoring were considered perfect for his new role and Dana's background in marketing would be helpful as well. The Turner's sending agency and Tim's supervisor in the host country were in favor of Tim's dual roles. Tim and Dana have three children: two boys and a girl; their youngest was born during their second year of sojourning. At present, Tim and Dana have been overseas for twenty-five years. Their children are in college in the U.S.

•••

Kelley Caldwell is a high school teacher who has worked for the past twenty years at a well-known international school. The school began as a service for the children of international workers, and still performs that function, but increasingly also serves diplomatic corps and international business personnel, as well as a growing number of host country parents who want their children to learn English. Kelley is single. At present she is considering taking a one year sabbatical to help her aging parents.

Spiritual Life

In chapter 8—about staying connected with God in the midst of storms—sojourners were encouraged to use brief and simple ways of maintaining habits of prayer and keeping God's Word in mind. Here is how long term international workers Tim and Dana Turner, and Kelley Caldwell, did in this area as they sojourned:

In their first six month of living overseas neither Tim nor Dana did very well at maintaining spiritual disciplines. They grew spiritually numb, and became more distant from each other as well, until they attended a retreat sponsored by their sending organization. At the retreat they experienced encouragement from others, learned simple ways to maintain connection with God and got back on track.

Since then, Tim, who is a morning person, has done well at having his devotions daily, first thing in the morning, most of the time. He loves to do in-depth book studies and have a leisurely time of prayer and worship. During times of stress or travel his devotional times are shorter, but for the most part, he has stuck to his routine. Somehow, talking with God and concentrating on scripture first thing, with a cup of coffee, works for him—even if it's only for a few minutes.

Dana is not a morning person and is less structured in her approach, but has committed to at least 15 minutes per day of reading a Psalm or favorite verse, even if it's the last thing she does at night. She works at staying connected to God throughout the day through short prayers, and trying to see any task as an act of worship. When life is not in upheaval, she spends an hour two or three mornings a week preparing for Bible studies or one-on-one discipleship meetings.

As a couple, Tim and Dana pray together several times a week—and more often during times of special need.

When the children were little, the family had times of daily Bible stories and prayer. As the children grew and got busier, family devotions evolved into three or four times per week with a changing format: sometimes they studied a book of the Bible, sometimes a topic, sometimes the biography of an inspirational Christian, sometimes the lyrics of music the kids chose.

While Tim and Dana continue their individualized spiritual disciplines per their personalities and styles, their prayer lives and commitment to God's Word are not compartmentalized to a few hours per day, but saturate everything they do. They are known among friends and colleagues for quoting scripture often, in their own words, and for singing songs of spiritual encouragement. When it is appropriate, they stop and pray for friends and colleagues on the spot, or send messages of prayer or spiritual encouragement.

Friends and acquaintances would say Tim and Dana quietly, consistently, practically, and compassionately live out what they say they believe.

•••

Kelley was disciplined about Bible study and prayer from the beginning of her sojourn, because she had learned in college and grad school how much she needed those disciplines. When she began to find Bible study and prayer a bit dry, she started memorizing and pondering chunks of scripture, creating imagery for the words in her mind. As a result, scripture became more alive for her. She also started singing hymns to God as worship.

As years have progressed, Kelley has varied the above approaches to maintaining her spiritual life, sometimes using one approach, often all of them. During times of high stress and little sleep she has found that her memorized verses and singing favorite hymns keep her spiritually anchored. In the last few years, she has helped start a Bible study with colleagues that they all enjoy.

If asked, Kelley would say that it is her ongoing spiritual life that has helped her remain sane overseas. Students and staff at her school would say Kelley is welcome in all settings because without being preachy she is always ready to provide practical help, a quiet prayer, or an encouraging scripture.

Evolving Identity

Figuring out who we are as we move to a new country, give up past roles and experience different degrees of being misunderstood was discussed in chapter 7. The challenges of knowing when and how to correct people's misperceptions and how to be content when we are misunderstood and feel like "nobody" were described. The truth that learning how to base our identity in Christ is critical for the long term health and effectiveness of the international worker was the main conclusion of chapter 7. As you will see from the stories of Kelley and the Turners, this task re-surfaces from time to time.

Because Kelley was a teacher before she moved overseas and continues to serve as a teacher, although in another country, she did not initially struggle with identity issues as much as sojourners whose role or job description changed more radically. But Kelley periodically wrestles with the fact that she herself sees her identity as so much more than a teacher. She thinks of the many adjustments she has made in order to live overseas: the complexities of dealing with multiple languages, currencies and cultures, for example. Then there are the other roles she has taken on: athletic coach, drama helper, leading discipleship groups, evangelizing, informal counseling… She feels that being seen as a teacher is accurate, but only captures the tip of the iceberg.

When she returns to the U.S. for home visits, Kelley feels even more acutely that people have an inadequate understanding of who she is. She would say a few people idealize her too much, as if she is some kind of hero—which Kelley disdains. Others seem unaware of how challenging it is to live overseas.

Kelley feels that few people, in the U.S. or in her adopted country, have a holistic or realistic view of who she really is. But when she feels hurt, lonely or devalued she has learned to intentionally take comfort from the fact that God knows and understands: he called her, he is the one she wants to please, and not being understood or appreciated is part of the vocation.

•••

Both Tim and Dana felt like misfits in their first year of sojourning: they felt incompetent in the language and knew their host country acquaintances had no idea what they had sacrificed to be there. Tim felt recognized as an agricultural professional, but the fact that he had been a well-loved pastor was unknown and unacknowledged. He felt like a huge part of him had been cut off. It felt to Tim and Dana like all relationships were superficial and it would take forever before they would be known, loved and appreciated as they had been at their church. The loneliness was acute and they felt like imposters.

But they kept praying about it, reminding each other of their previous sense of calling, and as they prayed, felt God wanted them to stay and keep trying. They stuck to their given roles and tried to wait with patience for relationships that would include discussions of faith. Gradually they got better at the language and even more gradually made friends. As Tim became more established in his professional roles and recognized in the community, he began to be asked to start small discipleship groups. Dana got involved at the school their children attended and found opportunities to lead Bible studies or prayer groups.

As life and ministries continued to evolve, however, both Tim and Dana had to continually rethink identity. The chance for Dana to use her professional skills in marketing never materialized and she eventually gave up on those hopes. At times she felt that she had no clear role or identity in anyone's mind—certainly not as a professional. But she was thankful to have the freedom to be involved in many activities and relationships that were accomplishing the goals they had started with. She decided to be content with that.

Tim's principle identity crisis came in their seventh year when two agricultural cooperatives imploded due to economic pressures and internal conflict—also affecting two related discipleship groups. Tim felt horrible. What happened was not his fault, but he felt like a failure and thought his reputation had been besmirched. He questioned who he was and what he was doing all over again. He had to let the two co-ops die and concentrated on helping the discipleship groups process and grieve. For himself, he sought out the counsel of godly men who had been through similar experiences. Gradually he was able to affirm anew the fact that he is God's child and servant; that his job is to serve as best he knows how and leave the results to God: his identity and worth are in God's hands.

In year #12, the Turners were asked to begin a new agricultural training center and co-op association in a different part of the country. This meant a move of 500 miles, learning a new tribal language and customs, and a change of schooling for their children. Tim and Dana's identities needed to adapt and change accordingly: they lost a network of friends and disciples who knew and understood them to a degree, and had to figure out all over again how to explain, or not explain, who they were, and wait with patience for a new network of relationships.

Today, Tim and Dana remain in that location. Both of them are well known and loved within their community: Tim as professor of agriculture and co-op specialist, but also as soccer coach for a local team and quiet leader of several groups of staunch disciples. Dana is known for helping schools excel at kids' clubs. It does not matter to them, now, that local friends have little awareness of who they were back in the U.S. or what they have sacrificed to live overseas.

But while their overseas identities are settled for the moment, Turners would agree with Kelley that every time they return to the U.S. for a visit they have to wrestle all over again with how much of their lives to try to explain, and have to work at being content with not being fully understood.

Retraining the Brain

Whenever we change locations or roles our brain has to re-learn the behavioral sequences that were so efficiently put on "automatic" in our previous life. And when we change cultures, our brain also has to become sensitive to the mostly unconscious assumptions about social interaction that drive the host culture. How to adjust to these challenging needs for retraining the brain was the topic of discussion in chapter 6. Let's see whether retraining their brains challenged Tim, Dana and Kelley only at the beginning of their sojourns or later on as well:

Because the language Tim and Dana needed to learn was recognized as difficult they were allowed to devote most of their first year overseas to language acquisition. But the agricultural college and co-ops were also anxious to get Tim involved. Learning a new language and culture, learning their way around and getting a household set up and functional, plus learning a new work environment stressed Tim and Dana to the maximum limit of their brain power. They were often exhausted and sometimes confused. At times they had to ask for time "off" away from all the stimulation to let their brains rest. They learned to spend time memorizing the words, cues or transactions they needed most. They also learned to compartmentalize certain times for working in English or the foreign language, and to confine calls from home to certain times per week.

They were blessed by having a colleague of Tim's who understood both the local culture and their American background so when they were stymied by awkward cultural misunderstandings, they could ask him and usually figure out what was going on.

By year three, Tim and Dana had many linguistic and logistical patterns on automatic pilot. They were also beginning to get a good handle on the underlying assumptions of their new culture. As Tim worked closely with his students, the co-ops and the fledgling disciple groups, he gained more and more insight into the values and customs of his host country in general and the particular tribal subculture of the area just outside the capitol city, where he and Dana lived and worked.

When Turners moved "up country" in their twelfth year and learned another tribal language, in some ways they had to start all over again: practicing language to get automaticity, learning their way around, building relationships. Some of the paradigms and assumptions of their new locale were similar to what they had already learned in the in the capitol city; others were different.

The biggest difference for Tim and Dana when they moved up country was that they knew how to learn: they embraced practicing verbs and vocabulary until they were automatic, made maps of their new city and outlying areas and diligently practiced learning their way around. They intentionally learned the names of tribal people by writing the names down on cards and memorizing. When they felt that awkward discomfort that is the clue that they were missing cultural cues, they missed being able to ask the friend they had had in the capitol city, but gradually learned who it was okay to ask or how to figure out what was going on.

As their kids have grown older, Tim and Dana have applied the same principles of brain retraining to understanding the music, vocabulary and technological domain common to their kids' generation. And each time they return to the U.S., Tim and Dana know they will have to embrace new technological ways of banking, shopping and communicating. When one of them balks at having to learn yet another new thing, they have learned to sigh, grin at each other and lean into it. Retraining the brain, they know, is a life-long necessity.

•••

Because Kelley's teaching role was so desperately needed at her international school, she was asked to begin living overseas without formal language learning. This made it hard for her, though, to shop, learn her way around and feel part of her host country community. She just worked, informally, at language and understanding the culture whenever she could. Finally, after her third year overseas, frustrated with not understanding the language and fitting in, she asked for, and was granted, a six month sabbatical for full-time language and cultural studies. This study helped her a great deal.

Because she was a teacher, Kelley was sensitive to her own learning style, applied the principles of automaticity. and learned the new language quickly. Because she already had some exposure to the culture, and many friendships among multi-cultural colleagues, students and parents, Kelley could ask questions about the cultural assumptions and paradigms that puzzled her.

Kelley loves to learn, and continues to study verbs and vocabulary in the foreign language. Whenever she suspects that a relational issue might have a cross-cultural cause, she works to figure out what is going on.

Kelley is also slowly working on an MA in counseling, since she finds she is often asked by students and parents to give advice. As she studies counseling, everything she has learned about automaticity, learning styles and cultural paradigms becomes more and more relevant. She finds herself helping others learn how to retrain their brains well, besides continually practicing the concepts herself.

Sabbath and Rest

The unique challenges of trying to find rest and create space for Sabbath amidst the challenges of living in a foreign culture and dealing with the endless demands of ministry were opened up in Chapter 5. Over against those challenges and demands were set the need to be obedient to God's design of Sabbath for his people, and his invitation to take time for rest by trusting him for the work he calls us to. Needless to say, Kelley and the Turners faced these challenges many times and in many ways.

As a young teacher, Kelley had plenty of energy and besides teaching a full load, got involved in coaching girls' soccer, teaching Bible studies and organizing school outings. She enjoyed it all, got to know many people and felt needed and fulfilled. When she felt tired she told herself she would rest during school vacations. But while school vacations provided a change of pace and activity, she found that she filled them with too much travel, visitors, or projects she hadn't had time for during the school year.

By year #5 Kelley felt exhausted and was ill most of her summer vacation. Reprimands from her doctor plus wise counsel from her pastor and his wife helped Kelley learn to build true Sabbath into her life. Depending on what is going on, she makes either Saturday or Sunday her day for restorative play, encouraging relationships, quiet rest—and worship. She now plans her vacations more carefully, and makes sure that at least two evenings a week are spent quietly at home.

•••

In their early years of language study the Turners were able to have a somewhat restful Sunday, although worship in the foreign language at first did little for them spiritually. They worked at having a date night for the two of them, and a family night of games and worship. But as Tim became involved at the training center, in the co-ops and then in discipleship groups, week days and week-ends became full. Soon he had almost no free time and became tired and frazzled. Everything he was doing was exciting and important and he could not figure out what to cut out. But Dana was becoming resentful of having all the family responsibilities fall on her, and no husband. Finally they took a week's vacation and used the time to rest, pray and think about what to do.

As a result, Tim talked with his supervisor and arranged to unobtrusively not work one morning and one afternoon per week. He used the morning "off" for a personal time of prayer, study and exercise and he and Dana used the afternoon time to share and pray together. They saved Friday evenings for family time.

By year #9, however, both Tim and Dana found themselves immersed in multiple roles in three ministries. Their Sabbath times had eroded as needs and schedules changed. Their kids were older and involved in more activities. There weren't many evenings or week-ends when the whole family was home; everyone was busy, busy, busy. Sabbath got forgotten.

When their oldest son was suspended for a serious infraction of school rules, it was a wake-up call for Tim and Dana. They realized they were way too busy, way too exhausted, and weren't giving enough attention to their kids, to each other—or to Sabbath. Both of them pulled out of one ministry role, scaled back on other roles, and together they made time for Sabbath, for intentional, quality time with each child, and for dates with each other.

Tim and Dana found that changes in their ministries, transitions between the school year and vacations and trips back and forth to the U.S. always upset their Sabbath and rest routines, but they learned to anticipate the changes and reconfigure commitments to make sure that rest, Sabbath, and quality time with God and each other remained a priority. This reconfiguring is a constant challenge, but when either Tim or Dana senses life is getting out of hand, they call a "marital meeting" and figure life out again. They have learned they don't like what happens when Sabbath gets squeezed out of their lives.

Recreation

Recreation—hobbies, exercise, play—are necessary for a healthy life and therefore should not be sacrificed as one builds a new life in a foreign country: that was the basic message of chapter 4. Recreational activities can also lay the groundwork for relationships and avenues of ministry. Tim, Dana and Kelley found this to be true in different ways.

Because of their commitment to a date night, Tim and Dana started, early in their sojourn, to explore different restaurants and doing so became great fun. For their family life, Tim and Dana planned evenings or days of games, movies or reading at home; at other times they took the kids to the local zoo. Tim coached the boys' soccer teams when they were in grade school, and that evolved, years later, into his being involved with the city's soccer league.

As the kids got older they tried camping, safaris and hikes as a family, with varying success, and finally landed on a strategy of two trips a year to the coast where they rented a beach house. The beach excursions seemed to work for every member of the family. Now that the kids are away in college, going to the beach is something they want to do whenever they "come home." Many wonderful memories were crafted there.

Besides couple and family recreation, Tim and Dana have learned that it helps them to have their own individual recreations: Tim gets his running in with the soccer team. Dana hates running, but exercises with one of her women's groups. She enjoys reading, collects paper backs from anywhere she can, and shares Kindle accounts with friends.

When their oldest son had his crisis, Tim and Dana realized they needed to work at doing something fun with the boys. Tim settled on purchasing two remote-controlled airplanes, and found places he and the boys could fly the planes. This worked well; one of the boys is now working towards his pilot's license. Dana, meanwhile, concentrated on sewing costumes for their daughter's drama club.

Now that their kids are away at college in the U.S. most of the year, Tim and Dana have reconfigured their recreational pursuits somewhat. Tim still runs and coaches soccer and Dana likes to read and exercises with her women's group, and they still love visiting restaurants, but they are trying to hike and walk together, too. Time will tell how well that works for them.

•••

Since Kelly loves all kinds of activities and works at an international school with multiple opportunities for hobbies and recreations, her challenge has been to narrow down choices to a few activities that meet her needs for exercise, friendship and renewal. Currently she runs with the girls on her volley ball team and plays tennis on week-ends. She took a class in pottery making and enjoys both the activity and companionship of others in the class. When she needs time alone—which even extrovert Kelley sometimes needs—she either reads or practices calligraphy. She has found doing the calligraphy restful, and it has the added bonus of concentrating her mind on scripture, since she often writes verses in beautiful script for herself or as gifts.

Loss and Grieving

We miss things, when we transfer to a new place, and have to learn to grieve what we miss, as discussed in chapter 3, or we won't have emotional space for new relationships and joys. Kelley and the Turners found this to be true in multiple transitions.

Kelley has found herself near tears often recently—ever since she learned of her mom's cancer diagnosis. Kelley knows her mom has a long battle ahead: surgery, chemo, and possibly a period of remission, but she fears she will eventually lose her mom, and hates being far away from her—especially right now. Kelley has already asked her director for a leave of absence as soon as classes are over so that she can be with her mom during the worst of the chemo and maybe longer. Kelley knows her current tears are from a combination of not being with her mom right now, plus some anticipatory grieving. Once she is with her mom and can be helpful she will be less emotional—until it is time to truly grieve.

But Kelley also knows that, if she must, she knows how to grieve: she has learned over the years to make time to listen to her own sadness or resentment due to losses, and allow herself to express those feelings in tears or words. Above all she knows she needs to pray it through: to be honest with God about her feelings, and open to receiving his comfort.

One of the things Kelley learned after year #3 of working at her school was that, paradoxically, she needed to make time for grieving after each school graduation. Graduation was a time of celebration—for the graduates, the school and teachers, of course. But after three years of waking up two days after graduation in a funk of depression, Kelley realized that the end of a school year signaled serious losses as well: students who were moving on, colleagues and friends who would not be returning. So she learned to allow several days for processing her grief at the end of every school year.

Every once in a while, also, Kelley feels a pang of homesickness from missing her family, or a wedding, birth, or holiday gathering. She has learned to lean into and experience the grieving, rather than pushing it away and pretending it isn't there.

Another loss Kelley has had to mourn is not being married. She didn't plan to be single, and hoped that Mr. Right would show up some day, but somehow he hasn't. Occasionally a possible mate appears on the horizon, and she has had some dates, only to find that there's not a good fit. Kelley has talked to the Lord about this issue often, sometimes with anger, sometimes with tears. She can go for weeks or even months at peace with the issue, but it seems that periodically she has to pray through her hopes, regrets and loss and arrive again at submission and trust in God's plan.

Because Kelley is honest about loss and has learned to do her grieving when she needs to, students and colleagues alike find her easy to talk to: she doesn't pretend life's losses don't hurt; but she doesn't wallow in self-pity either. She is sympathetic, but encouraging.

•••

Tim and Dana, at this stage of their lives, miss their college age kids—a lot. They work hard at staying in touch with them, and greatly look forward to any chance of being together as a family. They are also concerned for their aging parents, who are doing okay at the moment, but someday soon will need increasing help and eventually pass away. Neither of these losses causes deep grieving for Tim and Dana at present: missing their kids and concern for far away parents are just burdens they always carry and occasionally feel more deeply. When they feel particular pangs of sadness or worry they talk about them with each other, or pray about them. They know they will have grieving to do in the future, and they know how to do it.

Early in their first year of sojourn Tim and Dana missed their home church more than they thought possible, and their families, too. Each of them learned to make time alone to cry (in Dana's case), vent, journal and pray through the sense of loss they each felt. Sometimes they leaned on each other for support, but sometimes each of them was at a different point of grieving and did more of their thinking, praying or processing on their own.

In year #7 when Tim's two co-op groups imploded, he had to do quite a bit of grieving over the various losses involved in that situation. Dana supported him by listening a lot, understanding, giving him space and praying.

When the Turners moved up country, they were so busy for a while with all the logistics of moving and getting re-settled that they didn't realize they were also grieving the losses of friends, colleagues and familiarity that that move entailed—after all, they were still in the same country! Gradually they realized they had grieving to do and, each in their own way, grieved those losses.

Several years ago a family that had children the same ages as the Turners' kids left to return to the U.S. Dana and the wife and mom of that family had shared a strong friendship and many things in common. Dana grieved the loss of that friendship for a long time, and still misses her friend, at times acutely. They stay in touch via skype and social media, true, but it is not the same.

The Turners' kids have also had to grieve the loss of that family, and other losses involved in the moves and transitions the Turners have experienced. The family has evolved a sort of informal rule: when a family member seems out of sorts and it is likely due to a loss, that family member is allowed extra solitude, veg time, and grace. They know grieving is hard work, but has to be done.

Managing Stress

Stress just crops up now and then—sometimes overwhelmingly—and especially in cross-cultural living. When we are stressed we get sick more easily, can't sleep, can't think and in general…don't do well. That is why chapter 2 tackled the importance of learning to manage stress. Pacing ourselves, slowing ourselves down, allowing ourselves small breaks for relaxation and joy, getting a little bit of exercise, relaxing our muscles, breathing deeply—these are skills we need whenever we feel stressed—or see potential stress on the horizon.

As Tim, Dana and Kelley learned, they are good skills to have handy.

In their first months on the field, with two little children and a third on the way, Tim and Dana certainly experienced stress. Thanks to training they had received before they left the U.S., and to supportive colleagues, they learned to back off from too many commitments, rest when they were tired, and use the techniques that helped each of them de-stress. For Tim this involved making time for running, doing progressive muscle relaxation and watching sports on TV. Dana learned to leave the kids in Tim's hands or with a friend and curl up with a book, write in her journal or go on a shopping expedition.

As time went on Tim and Dana occasionally didn't realize that stress was mounting up until they got grumpy, snapped at each other, or one of them got sick. Then they remembered to use the coping skills that worked best for each of them.

As they got older, they learned to look ahead and when they saw a time of stress coming up, they planned for extra down time, before, after or during the stress. They encouraged each other to make time for reading or exercise. Tim found that when he had a great deal of desk work he would get tense. At those times especially, exercise and progressive muscle relaxation helped. Dana found herself keyed up and anxious before leading Bible studies or women's retreats, even though she loved doing so, and learned to breathe deeply before events to prevent stress, and after, to recover.

The Turner family found that during any transition—preparing to go back to the U.S., or returning to the field, or getting ready for the school year or a big trip—they needed to watch out for stress symptoms and plan to de-stress. Sometimes they declared a family pajama day: everyone stayed home and relaxed; or certain family members did so.

At one point, during year #11, the Turners' adopted country experienced political strife: demonstrations, shootings, unrest, threats. Dana was attacked while driving in the car alone and their house was broken into. The attack, the robbery and the general upheaval caused considerable tension and anxiety for the whole family. They practiced deep breathing and progressive muscle relaxation together, as well as special times of prayer and reading God's promises. Dana found that she needed to use deep breathing and muscle relaxation exercises several times a day, plus she needed extra rest and solitude. After several months of political disquiet, Tim and Dana talked with their leadership and purposely left the country for two weeks of vacation, to de-stress and get restored. When they returned, both the country, and they themselves, were calmer. The Turners know, though, that such unrest could recur.

In spite of past stress and loss, Tim and Dana feel fulfilled in their work and delighted in the relationships and growth of faith happening around them. They know there will be more stress and loss ahead, but they are confident in the God who has called them and met their needs so far. As they drift off to sleep one of them will often ask the other, "Anyone you know that you would trade lives with?" "Nope, no way," the other answers.

•••

Early in her sojourn Kelley was stressed by all the usual challenges of adjusting to a foreign country and a new school. In the midst of all that stress she also tried to stay in touch with family and friends in the U.S. on a daily basis and didn't get enough sleep. Needless to say, she became worn out, grumpy and jumpy. After a month of that, she learned to be honest with her family and friends in the U.S. about how little time she could spend online or on the phone. She set clear expectations for herself and for them about how often she could skype, chat or talk. As a result, her stress level went down.

Over the years Kelley has learned to recognize the times of the school year that are typically stressful for her and to be sure to get enough sleep, solitude, exercise, and time doing relaxing things—like her calligraphy. She finds, for example, that the month before the Christmas holidays is always stressful. Usually there are sports events, concerts, dramas and a rush of papers and grades to turn in. It is all worthwhile and most of it is fun, but she has learned to keep her evenings alone sacrosanct, and to practice deep breathing and do yoga stretches when she gets agitated or tense. She also keeps the two days after school closes for the holidays for "absolutely nothing," so that she can recover.

Kelley generally likes her life very much, and feels she is serving her Lord in just the way He has called her to do. She knows she needs to manage stress, rest and stay close to the Lord to be able to continue at the school, and in the country she has come to love—even after whatever happens with her mom.

About the Author

Connie Befus, Ph.D., grew up in Africa and has also lived in Central and South America. Crossing cultures, and watching others struggle in cross-cultural adaptation led her to do her doctoral dissertation research on culture shock. She has used her research, her experience overseas and her expertise as a psychologist to train, counsel and encourage cross-cultural workers for over 35 years. She loves to help people integrate truths from God's word and the practice of spiritual disciplines with appropriate psychological research and techniques—for healthy, vibrant lives and service.

CPSIA information can be obtained
at www.ICGtesting.com
Printed in the USA
LVHW02s1343090318
569266LV00001BA/1/P